STUDIES IN ECONOMIC AND SOCIAL HISTORY

This series, specially commissioned by the Economic History Society, provides a guide to the current interpretations of the key themes of economic and social history in which advances have recently been made or in which there has been significant debate.

Originally entitled 'Studies in Economic History', in 1974 the series had its scope extended to include topics in social history, and the new series title, 'Studies in Economic and Social History', signalises this development.

The series gives readers access to the best work done, helps them to draw their own conclusions in major fields of study, and by means of the critical bibliography in each book guides them in the selection of further reading. The aim is to provide a springboard to further work rather than a set of pre-packaged conclusions or short-cuts.

ECONOMIC HISTORY SOCIETY

The Economic History Society, which numbers over 3000 members, publishes the *Economic History Review* four times a year (free to members) and holds an annual conference. Enquiries about membership should be addressed to the Assistant Secretary, Economic History Society, Peterhouse, Cambridge. Full-time students may join at special rates.

STUDIES IN ECONOMIC AND SOCIAL HISTORY

Edited for the Economic History Society by L. A. Clarkson

PUBLISHED

OTHER TITLES IN PREPARATION

The Economic Effects of the American Civil War

Prepared for
The Economic History Society by

PATRICK K. O'BRIEN

Reader in Economic History and
Professorial Fellow of
St Antony's College, Oxford

MACMILLAN
EDUCATION

First published 1988

Published by
MACMILLAN EDUCATION LTD
Houndmills, Basingstoke, Hampshire RG21 2XS
and London
Companies and representatives
throughout the world

Printed in Hong Kong

ISBN 0-333-38818-6

Series Standing Order

If you would like to receive future titles in this series as they are
published, you can make use of our standing order facility. To place a
standing order please contact your bookseller or, in case of difficulty,
write to us at the address below with your name and address and the
name of the series. Please state with which title you wish to begin your
standing order. (If you live outside the UK we may not have the rights
for your area, in which case we will forward your order to the publisher
concerned.)

Customer Services Department, Macmillan Distribution Ltd
Houndmills, Basingstoke, Hampshire, RG21 2XS, England.

Contents

Acknowledgements

My interest in the economic history of the United States was first aroused by two stimulating teachers of the subject at the London School of Economics, Charlotte Ericson and Jim Potter. Over the years it has been kept alive because no European historian can ignore the vanguard of his discipline. I have also enjoyed the friendship and encouragement of distinguished practitioners of the field, including: Robert Fogel, Bob Gallman, John James, Lance Davis, Bill Parker and Richard Sylla. During a semester at Princeton my colleagues Jim Oakes and Michael Feldman made me read more political history. Above all this essay owes any merit it displays to the patient, constructive and remorseless criticism of that great economic historian and true gentleman, Stanley Engerman. If mistakes and misinterpretations remain they occur because I have ignored his advice.

Note on References

References in the text within square brackets relate to the numbered items in the Bibliography, followed, where necessary, by the page numbers in italics, for example [1, 7–9].

Editor's Preface

When this series was established in 1968 the first editor, the late Professor M. W. Flinn, laid down three guiding principles. The books should be concerned with important fields of economic history; they should be surveys of the current state of scholarship rather than a vehicle for the specialist views of the authors, and above all, they were to be introductions to their subject and not 'a set of pre-packaged conclusions'. These aims were admirably fulfilled by Professor Flinn and by his successor, Professor T. C. Smout, who took over the series in 1977. As it passes to its third editor and approaches its third decade, the principles remain the same.

Nevertheless, times change, even though principles do not. The series was launched when the study of economic history was burgeoning and new findings and fresh interpretations were threatening to overwhelm students – and sometimes their teachers. The series has expanded its scope, particularly in the area of social history – although the distinction between 'economic' and 'social' is sometimes hard to recognise and even more difficult to sustain. It has also extended geographically; its roots remain firmly British, but an increasing number of titles is concerned with the economic and social history of the wider world. However, some of the early titles can no longer claim to be introductions to the current state of scholarship; and the discipline as a whole lacks the heady growth of the 1960s and early 1970s. To overcome the first problem a number of new editions, or entirely new works, have been commissioned – some have already appeared. To deal with the second, the aim remains to publish up-to-date introductions to important areas of debate. If the series can demonstrate to students and their teachers the importance of the discipline of economic and social history and excite its further study, it will continue the task so ably begun by its first two editors.

The Queen's University of Belfast   L. A. CLARKSON
                                                      General Editor

7

Editor's Preface

1 Counterfactual Speculations

Between 1776 and 1914 real income per head in the United States probably multiplied more than six times. As the economy developed, the share of total output which was agricultural in form diminished markedly and the proportion of the labour force engaged in agriculture, forestry and fishing declined from over three-quarters at the time of the Revolution to less than a third by 1910 [118, 95, 98; 87, 181]. Observing that the long transition to ever higher standards of living did not proceed smoothly or continuously, historians have segmented this process, called structural change, into swings and shorter cycles of faster and slower rates of change. Interruptions to economic progress associated with falling levels of investment, runs of poor harvests and depressed world trade, meant that modern economic growth was (and continues to be) anything but a steady process. On several occasions war also intervened to influence the pace and pattern of economic advance. Americans found themselves in conflict with other nations several times. War with Britain attended the creation of the United States from 1776–83. War maintained the republic's independence from 1812–15. War with Mexico, 1846–8, extended its territory by thousands of square miles. Above all, war kept the young country together after a bloody civil conflict between North and South.

There is no comparison between the sums expended by the Federal and Confederate governments on armed struggle from 1861–5 and the costs shouldered by Americans of earlier generations to achieve and retain sovereignty. The Civil War remains the 'greatest event' in American history. Its causes and consequences are an enduring concern for scholars, and economic historians have entertained three general hypotheses on connections between the Civil War and the long-run progress of the American economy. First, that it interrupted the secular boom underway before hostilities commenced and which would have

9

continued at constant (or even accelerated) rates of growth; secondly (and because there are sound reasons to expect 'booms' to tail off) the war had only a marginal impact upon the long-term development of the United States; and, thirdly, that the Civil War obviated potential bottlenecks to growth and over time sustained even higher rates of development than would have been the case without armed conflict between North and South. Possibilities considered range from positive through neutral to negative effects. Although the Civil War did not arrest the onward march of their economy, the task of this essay is to survey recent attempts by American economic historians to define, analyse and measure its impact on the *long-run* rate of economic progress of the United States. That task will not be easy, basically because the question pushes discussion towards counterfactual arguments about the plausible pace and pattern of economic growth without war. Furthermore, it is neither logical nor feasible to separate the effects of war, *per se*, from the effects of slave emancipation and the reconstruction of Southern institutions which followed directly from the military defeat of the Confederacy. As usual, the information which has been established and well reviewed by American historians is scarce or of poor quality. (The data on sources are reviewed in [64, *126–30*].) Facts are difficult enough to establish without speculating on what might have happened. Nevertheless, counterfactual reasoning is implicit in the question because to investigate the probable effects of war involves, by implication, an enquiry into the likely growth path of the United States hypothetically untroubled by civil strife or by the need to adjust to the abolition of slavery in the South.

2   Direct Costs and Economic Causes of the Civil War

Before turning to studies concerned with the impact of war on long-run development, it will be useful to consider first the published estimates of the direct costs of the war for American society. Relevant figures have been extracted from budgets which recorded governmental expenditures in wartime and during the transition to peace. These estimates exclude civil expenditures unconnected with war and the costs of maintaining a military establishment in peacetime. Here the normal assumption made is that in the absence of war the costs of the armed services would have remained constant. Incremental costs, expressed in dollars, are then deemed to measure the immediate burden imposed on American society, contingent upon the reallocation of resources from civilian to military purposes and back again. Thus the figures in Table 1 represent the 'price' paid to transform 'butter into guns'.

Another tangible cost of war which has been measured is the value of productive capital destroyed by enemy action. Official statistics also recorded the numbers of men, women and children killed or wounded in the course of conflict, who suffered death or who were disabled as a consequence of events related to the war. While it is crass to put a price on life and injury, economic historians (and insurance companies) have valued human losses in terms of the output potentially produced or incomes potentially earned over the lifetimes of Americans killed and wounded during the conflict.

Figures set out in Table 1 are not easy to comprehend. Rows A and B represent the 'consumption foregone' by Americans of the North and South as a consequence of taxation, borrowing, direct expropriation and other fiscal actions taken by their governments to finance warfare. The estimates have been formulated from the perspective of citizens alive on the eve of Civil War when consumption per capita came to about $120 a year. We could say that (on average) fiscal expropriations for war cost Americans

Table 1   The Direct Costs of Civil War

	Totals	Per head
	(In $ of 1861)	
1. Military costs		
A. War expenditures and expropriations by Federal, state and local governments of the North	$2.3 billion	$98
B. War expenditures and expropriations by Confederate, state and local governments of the South	$1.0 billion	$111
2. The destruction of capital		
C. The North	—	
D. The South	$1.49 billion	
3. Human losses		
E. 360,000 Union soldiers killed	$955 million	
275,175 Union soldiers wounded	$365 million	
F. 258,000 Confederate troops killed	$684 million	
197,000 Confederate troops wounded	$261 million	

Notes: $ of 1861 means that governmental expenditures on war through time, the estimated loss of earnings (caused by death and wounding) through time and the value of capital destroyed in the South have been discounted to dollars of 1861. The discount rate used to express future values in terms of present values of 1861 was 6 per cent.

Sources: [49, *305–26*].

roughly the equivalent of one year's consumption. 'Burdens of war' should also be interpreted in terms of capacity to pay and thus related to national income assuming at least for purposes of the argument pursued here that national income has been estimated within tolerable bounds of accuracy. (Discussions of American national income estimates are in [81, *3–117*; 15, *154–95*].) To fund their Civil War the Federal and Confederate governments expropriated real resources valued at 1.2 times the income of the whole country for 1861. Over the war period Union and Confederate armies 'consumed' 20–25 per cent of their nation's annual income while engaged in destroying and damaging human and physical capital worth nearly $4 billion.

Post hoc, what is more poignant is that the cost of armed conflict turns out to be far larger than any sum hypothetically required to compensate slaveowners for the value of their slaves. Claudia Goldin has calculated that an emancipation scheme designed to compensate white Southerners at real market values for their 'human property', and spread over three decades of Federal budgets, could have cost *all* American taxpayers just $7.25 a year (in prices of 1860). That represented a mere 5 per cent of their per capita incomes at that time although a far larger proportion of Federal tax revenue [48, *73–5*]. (On the political viability of proposals for compensated emancipation see [35, 170–85].) Of course the offer would have been refused, but looked at with hindsight we now can appreciate by how much the Civil War did not pay for anyone, and especially for white Southerners. By 1866 3.8 million slaves had been emancipated without compensation. Aggregate costs of the decision to go to war for *free white Southerners* amounted to: slaves worth $2.7 billion, plus $1.0 billion of military expenditures as well as the costs of damaged people and property— which adds up to something over $6.0 billion (see Table 1). And this huge sum does not include the decline in Southern land values which also flowed directly from the abolition of slavery. Although that $6 billion was not spread evenly over the 6.37 million white population of the Confederacy, as an approximation it may have been equal to a loss of assets worth about $942 per white Southerner (in 1860 prices). Just before the war incomes among whites in the South averaged $125. Given that the white South lost at least $6 billion of its stock of human and physical capital and again selecting 6 per cent as the model rate of return on fairly safe investments, the direct economic impact of war (including uncompensated emancipation) on the incomes of *white Southerners* can be represented as equivalent to a drastic reduction of something like 44 per cent in their incomes, per capita, for 1860. For Northerners the comparable loss was nothing like as onerous: a mere $164 a head. Expressed as a capital sum and capitalised at 6 per cent this yields under $10 a year – which represents only 7 per cent of average incomes in the North for 1860 [49, *304, 308, 323–6*; 48, 73–9].

Why then did Americans fight each other when the outcome

proved so expensive for all concerned? Although they are now more preoccupied with effects than causes, economic historians have contributed something to the continuing debate on the *origins* of Civil War. First, they quantified the economic interest of Southern whites in the *status quo*. Slavery was a profitable and viable institution. Just how profitable and viable for how long continues to be controversial, but there is now almost no support for the traditional view that on the eve of the Civil War slavery was in danger of immediate collapse under the momentum of its own inherent inefficiency. On the contrary, the increase in European demand for cotton grown in the South generated conditions in which the real incomes of whites had increased sharply over the first half of the nineteenth century. It seems that for decades before the war only temporary and short-term downswings interrupted the upward march of Southern prosperity and average real incomes for free whites rose by about 43 per cent between 1840–60. Over the longer period from 1800–60 cotton output had grown at around 6 per cent a year. Sugar production increased at a comparable rate while the long-term rates of growth for rice and tobacco probably proceeded at just under 3 per cent per annum. In retrospect it was the golden age of an *ancien régime* and the 1850s were accurately perceived by Southerners as their greatest boom [118, *237–43*]; but see [44, *1009–13*].

Table 2   The Composition of Wealth in Five Cotton States, 1860

Asset	Value in millions of dollars	Percentage of total wealth
Slaves	1589	45.8
Farmlands and buildings	868	25.0
Farm animals	172	5.0
Farm implements	48	1.4
Manufacturing capital	38	1.1
Other real estate	364	10.5
Other assets	393	11.3
Total	3472	100.00

Source: [90, *12*]. The five states are: South Carolina, Georgia, Alabama, Mississippi and Louisiana.

Table 3 The Loss of Income to Free Citizens in the Slave States from Non-compensated Abolition of Slavery in 1860

State	Per capita income	Percent slave	Slave earnings per free citizen	Earnings other than from slaves per free citizen	Percent reduction in income of free citizens from abolition
	$		$	$	
Alabama	75	45	50	70	42
South Carolina	80	57	57	102	36
Florida	89	44	48	95	34
Georgia	84	44	40	96	29
Mississippi	125	55	74	179	29
Louisiana	131	47	54	175	24
Texas	(100)	30	26	108	24
Above 7 states	97	46	50	113	31
North Carolina	79	33	21	87	19
Tennessee	75	25	17	76	18
Arkansas	95	26	21	100	17
Virginia	88	32	20	100	17
Above 11 states	91	38	35	100	23
Kentucky	83	19	10	88	10
Maryland	(90)	13	6	94	6
Missouri	(90)	10	5	93	5

Note: The loss excludes the fall in land values contingent upon emancipation. Wiener [122, 13] cites estimates of a 50 per cent decline.
Source: (54, 922).

At the beginning of the nineteenth century the average output of cotton per slave sold for $17.47. By 1860 cotton output per slave had increased about five times and the average price of a prime field hand had risen from around $600 in 1800 to about $1800 six decades later [55, 242–53]. Like other income-producing assets (capital goods) the price of slaves rose with the predicted value of their output [12, 47–66, 75–8]. Throughout the South something like 40 per cent of free whites owned slaves from whom they derived a substantial fraction of their disposable incomes and the

15

ownership of slaves represented a high proportion of Southern wealth. Ransom and Sutch have published estimates of the composition of wealth in five cotton states for 1860 and Gunderson has calculated the share of per capita income derived by all free white citizens from the ownership and exploitation of slave labour (see Tables 2 and 3 above).

Clearly their pecuniary interest was widespread and had appreciated rapidly over the 1850s when the selling price of field hands doubled in anticipation of further and increasing profits from the sales of cotton and other primary produce on world markets. Right up to the war, capital gains continued to accrue to slaveholders large and small. They formed a class with a coherent economic interest not only in the preservation of slavery but also in suppressing views that diminished expectations about the long-run viability of that inhumane institution. Property values (as every homeowner knows) depend upon buyers' anticipations of long-term stability in political, legal and other arrangements affecting the sale and purchase of houses. When the Federal government seemed to threaten the security of their most important property right Southerners found secession from the Union an increasingly attractive way to preserve its value [54, *915–29*; 39, *93–4, 103–6*].

In marked contrast to the South, and despite venerable historians who have argued the contrary case, it is difficult to discern the economic interest of the North in armed conflict. (For the contrary and traditional views of Beard, Hacker and Miller see [106, *396–400*; 28, *370–1*].) Political divisions between representatives of the two regions over tariffs, land settlement, banking, transportation and other categories of Federal policy, represented minor and far from generalised clashes of interest, which were, in any case, not consistently resolved in favour of one or other of the two contending groups of states [136, *130–9*]. In prospect no economic gains appeared to accrue to citizens of the North from emancipation. Indeed dominant political groups (and perhaps a majority of voters) in the North were not in favour of abolition. Almost nobody (except extreme abolitionists) would have wished to free slaves without compensation [35, *170*]. Although Congress discussed emancipation proposals with compensation and in 1862 Lincoln looked at some calculations, the issue was never seriously considered [48, *73–9*; 136, *136–7*; 14, *7–10*]. And Gunderson's suggestion that the North preferred war to compensation because (before hostilities commenced) the former 'seemed' a cheaper alternative to Northern taxpayers has little to recommend it [54, *915–45*].

Both sides seriously miscalculated the ultimate costs of armed conflict. Most Southerners never expected the North to wage total war to defend the Union let alone to free slaves. For them secession was perceived as a regrettable but necessary way to safeguard property values embodied in slaves and not as a step on the road to an expensive combat [136, *146–7*; 79, *16–23*]. On these occasions (as history so sadly shows) blunder is inevitable. Time spans and costs of war are normally underestimated by politicians who manage crises. Not only was the American Civil War no exception but, in retrospect, it has the distinction of being the first 'modern war', fought on an unprecedented scale by some 2 million soldiers, and supplied by governments with more resources, organisational capacity and technology at their disposal than anything Napoleon could command half a century earlier. At the finish, this first major war of the Industrial Era turned out to be colossally expensive for all concerned. Only freed slaves really gained. And to the *long-run costs* of the conflict this survey now returns.

3 Long-run Costs of War

Counterfactual speculation is unavoidable because the long-term costs of civil war must be separated from other (and often far more significant) forces operating upon the growth of the economy. Yet there is certainly no mistaking the war's *immediate* impact on growth rates for America's national product and real per capita income from 1860–70. Both rates slumped markedly below trend values. They then accelerated over the following decade as recovery and regeneration carried the economy forward again [118, *98*; 87, *188*] No surprise will be occasioned by the discovery that the dislocation, disruption and destruction contingent upon civil war, and the reallocation of manpower and other resources back to normal employment after the termination of hostilities, reduced the capacity of the American economy to maintain steady growth in the production of goods and services. Neither is it particularly illuminating to point to the phase of rapid recovery after Lee's surrender. Proceeding from an artificially depressed level and with a backlog of investment and innovations to undertake, economies have often recovered from war at a rapid pace [53, *173–80*].

Thus connections between mobilisation and demobilisation for war on the one hand and economic growth on the other raise no particular problems for economic history. But it seems far more difficult to specify and to estimate the long-run gains and losses operating upon the economy for several decades after the termination of any war [71, *69–93*; 72, *35*]. Some things can in principle be measured. For example, military action destroys or damages the capacity of labour and capital to produce future flows of output. Such effects are not usually prolonged through time and, given information on the expected life of workers and of machines at the moment of destruction, it may be possible to calculate the value of production lost through warfare. More permanent losses attend ecological destruction. Fortunately (and

18

Sherman's infamous march notwithstanding) natural resources, particularly land and mineral deposits, were not easily destroyed by pre-nuclear and pre-chemical warfare. But as the result of war, wealth could be lost for ever through enforced transfers of territory between sovereign states. Access to markets, raw materials and other imports could be denied to vanquished nations and second-best solutions to such restraints on trade and production imposed costs on losers and represented material benefits for victors. In principle, a list of gains and losses (imputable to war and peace treaties) may be tabulated, perhaps estimated as a negative or positive percentage of a nation's long-term rate of growth. In the modern era of economic development these effects diminished through time as an ever-growing increment to national output in absolute terms swamped the fixed losses or gains of output contingent upon wars fought decades before. More problematical to identify, and almost impossible to estimate, are a range of economic effects which flow from changes in attitudes and values, from reforms to property rights, institutions and laws, which can be connected with warfare and its political settlements and which for a long time have dominated discussions of the economic consequences of both the English and American civil wars [109, 24–62; 106, 396–400].

Imputation and measurement seem so intrinsically difficult to handle empirically that some historians prefer to make the reasonable assumption that in the absence of war economies would continue to grow at some specified pre-bellum rate of advance. They then define the observed difference in consumption per head between hypothetical growth at the pre-war rate and the actual levels of per capita consumption achieved over war and post-war periods—as the loss or gain to populations from war. Such calculations do not provide anything like accurate measures of the long-run costs of wars but they do generate rough estimates and push discussion in the right direction.

In this context such numbers purport to measure the deprivation attributable to the Civil War as experienced by Americans, resident North and South of the Mason–Dixon line and as expressed in terms of reduced levels of real consumption per person through time. That deprivation (represented as the percentage difference from unobserved but counterfactual levels of consumption) rises to a maximum during the conflict and then

Table 4 Estimated Losses in Consumption per Head, Notionally Impu:·ed to the Civil War

	USA		North		South	
	Loss in $ (a)	Loss as a % (b)	Loss in $ (a)	Loss as a % (b)	Loss in $ (a)	Loss as a % (b)
1861	8	7	5	4	12	16
1862	13	12	11	9	23	35
1863	20	19	15	12	32	55
1864	25	25	20	17	41	82
1865	31	32	24	21	48	181
1869	27	25	19	15	49	102
1874	19	16	10	7	46	88
1879	13	9	—	—	48	77
1884	13	8	—	—	51	73
1889	12	8	—	—	47	70
1894	11	7	—	—	43	66
1899	12	6	—	—	49	62
1904	13	7	—	—	52	58
1909	14	6	—	—	57	54

(a) 'Loss' is expressed in absolute and real terms in dollars of 1860. That loss is equal to the gap between hypothetical and observed per capita consumption streams – calculated on the assumption that real per capita income in 'warless' America would continue to grow at the pre-war (1839–59) rates of 1.56 per cent for the North and 1.30 per cent for the South until 1909. Loss means that each citizen of the North and South consumed less than they would have done if the Civil War had not occurred.

(b) Loss is expressed as a percentage of *actual* per capita consumption. For example, the table 'purports' to say that without Civil War and its contingent peace settlement per capita consumption in the South in 1909 could have been as high as $162 a head or 54 per cent above the observed level.

Source: [49, *309–20*].

decreased in percentage terms as the American economy reverted to normal peacetime economic growth.

By 1914 the economic burden of the war spread over the entire population of the United States had diminished almost to insignificance. For residents of the Northern States the costs of preserving Union rose to a maximum of $24 per head in 1865 and then declined rapidly. On the assumptions specified, Northerners' burdens had disappeared by 1879 when actual and 'counterfactual' levels of per capita consumption became identical.

4 The Long-run Costs of Civil War for the South

For those who resided in the South the immediate costs and long-term burdens of the Civil War remained way above anything experienced by their Yankee enemies. Thus the Confederacy, which contained 27 per cent of America's population and received 20 per cent of the national income, suffered 65 per cent of the costs (short- and long-term) of the Civil War [49, 232–6]. In Table 4 that cost has been spread across the entire population of the South, white and black. For whites alone the long-term costs of war and emancipation represented an enormous and persistent loss of real income. No wonder the Civil War is still regarded as a major catastrophe for the South and its legacy of bitterness and racism prevailed for more than a century.

But calculations of its burden boldly presented in Table 4 are not 'facts'. Those figures are merely 'numbers' generated by one critical assumption: that without the Civil War slavery would have survived and economic growth in the South would have proceeded at the rates estimated for 1839–59. The results of such calculations are 'useful fictions' because they help to make concrete otherwise vague notions about the economic effects of war. They focus discussion on critical assumptions which generate estimates. They structure arguments around attempts to refine and rank the important magnitudes involved. For example, several scholars have attacked the premise that high growth rates observed from 1839–59 were sustainable over the long run. Other historians are inclined to derogate the significance of the Civil War because, as they argue, the observed rates of growth achieved by the South from 1870 to 1914 seem satisfactory and on a par with the rest of the United States. Another group point to the impossibility of separating the effects of war from the demise of slavery which they argue would have been abolished sooner or later anyway.

Thus our first problem resides in comparing statistics related to
long-term growth on a regional basis. Net national product per
capita is the preferred index for computing changes in average
standards of living over time. Unfortunately, rates of growth for
the North and the South measured by that indicator are not
available down to 1914. But for two decades before the war per
capita incomes in the South increased by 39 per cent compared to
29 per cent for the North and 33 per cent for the United States as a
whole. By the outbreak of hostilities per capita income in the
relatively backward South had risen to reach 80 per cent of the
national average, while the per capita income level enjoyed by the
region's *free* men, women and children was marginally above the
level enjoyed by free citizens of the North [37, *335*; 29, *351–6*].
These rates differ slightly from those found in [49]; see also [44,
1009–12]. Southern incomes plummeted during the war, recovered in the 1870s and attained by 1880 a standard little better
than the level of four decades earlier. At that point in the
nineteenth century Southern per capita incomes had declined to
about half the national average. The region remained in this
unenviable position until after 1900 when its rate of advance
accelerated so that by 1920 incomes reached about 62 per cent of
the all-American average [27, *528*]. On the basis of this data the
long-run economic growth of the South can be depicted as:
exceptionally rapid growth for the two decades before secession:
followed by the catastrophe of the Civil War (when commodity
output per capita declined by 39 per cent) [28, *371–2*; 99, *31*]. For
the rest of the century per capita income indeed grew at around the
national rate. Although the Southern economy was clearly not
stagnant before 1914, it suffered from conspicuous backwardness
compared to the North. Whatever potential the slave economy of
the old South possessed for growth (and that potential seemed
particularly strong from 1840–60) had been severely damaged.
War, defeat and the abrupt termination of slavery apparently
depressed average incomes well below the relative economic status
exhibited by the region in 1840. Thereafter possibilities for
'catching up' with the rest of America depended on sustaining a
long-run rate of growth of income per capita *well above* the national

average – in fact above 3 per cent a year – a seemingly impossible task for an economy and society devastated and disheartened by total war.

The 'South' which fought the Civil War included 11 states and it is possible to narrow the focus to subregions of the Confederacy. In their celebrated study Ransom and Sutch selected a 5-state region (South Carolina, Georgia, Alabama, Mississippi and Louisiana) to represent the major cotton producers and plantation economies of the old South. Before the war slaves, who comprised roughly half the population of these 5 states, provided free citizens with more than a third of their incomes. Together with Florida they formed the so-called Gulf Squadron and seceded from the Union almost immediately after Lincoln's election as President. For these 'plantation economies' secession turned into an economic disaster. Between 1859–67 crop output per member of the rural population declined from $85 to $38 and it failed to reach its peak level for the rest of the nineteenth century. On this type of index and down to 1914 the 'Deep South' perhaps never recovered from Civil War and Emancipation. Assuming that the rate of growth of crop output per capita is a reasonable proxy for the growth rate of real per capita income, then between 1869–73 and 1902–6 real incomes in the *Deep South* apparently progressed at less than half the observed rate for the United States as a whole [92, *9–12, appdx A*; 94, *213–22*].

For the 'Gulf Squadron' military defeat led to a severe drop in income and retardation for the rest of the nineteenth century. Other states of the Confederacy seem to have recovered more quickly and to have grown thereafter more rapidly. But their experience has not been analysed in anything like the same depth and sophistication. And the 'optimistic' interpretation of their long-run development has been derived from estimates of regional per capita income which may be less secure than an index based on crop output, preferred by Ransom and Sutch. (Engerman [31, *7–9*] disputes their data but Ransom and Sutch [94, *213–22*] are not disposed to rely on regional accounts.) Perhaps, also, the states of Virginia, North Carolina, Kentucky, Tennessee and Texas possessed a greater capacity for structural transformation and performed better than the Deep South because, after the Civil War, they moved further and faster away from an agrarian economy [74, *31–8*].

23

Clearly the speed of recovery and the persistence of retardation varied between subregions of the South. Aggregation is permissible simply to generalise about the effects of war on a defeated Confederacy. Between 1860–70 its per capita income fell by nearly 40 per cent. There followed a decade of recovery when income per capita rose by 29 per cent. But from 1880 to 1910, although average income grew at the national rate, the Southern economy never caught up with the North and an income differential between South and North opened up from a position of around 80 per cent in 1860 (and, narrowing by the year) to 58 per cent in 1870 – which is roughly where it remained for the rest of the century.

(ii) PROBLEMS OF SOUTHERN BACKWARDNESS

Most of the fall in Southern output over the 1860s can be attributed directly to the calamitous effects of war fought on its terrain. What seems far more difficult to explain is slow growth in the Deep South and the persistent backwardness of the South as a whole. Why did it fail to regain its relative economic status with the North? Ignoring the explicable period of recovery, after the war, why did the growth of per capita income in the South fall consistently and appreciably below the performance the region achieved before 1860? How far did Civil War, post-war reconstruction and the emancipation of slaves arrest the capacity of the South for long-term development? The numbers already cited (in Table 4) should help us to think more cogently about these big questions.

They suggest that without the Civil War, and *if* the South had continued to grow at the pre-war (1839–59) rate of advance, then between 1861 and 1909 per capita real consumption could have been sustained some 40 to 50 per cent above observed levels. Behind this estimated 'loss of consumption' lies a 'Counterfactual South'; a region untouched by the devastation of war, where slavery survives, plantations are not broken up, institutions are not 'reconstructed' and international demand for cotton continues to expand at the rapid rates enjoyed by Southerners for decades before secession.

Just to expose the assumptions behind the stylised facts in the table raises almost all major arguments about the long-run impact of civil war on the South. How serious was destruction from a war fought largely on Southern territory? How long could slave plantations have survived? What effects on economic growth should be imputed to their break up and to the emancipation of black slaves – perhaps an inevitable change, with or without war? What connections can be traced between the attempts of the Federal government to reconstruct the Southern economy after the war and its performance down to 1914? Finally, was world demand for cotton destined to grow at a constant rate to 1914? These questions implicitly separate the legacies of slavery, war, emancipation and reconstruction and raise insoluble methodological problems for this survey. Historians will agree that slavery in America had to end some time before the twentieth century but when and how becomes crucial for any assessment of the costs of the Civil War which did, in fact, bring about abolition more than twenty years before the emancipation of Cuban and Brazilian slaves. (For a discussion of emancipation and limits to the survival of slavery in the New World see [32, 192–5].) The final question also distinguishes the impact of war from the growth in international demand for cotton. Manufacturing industries normally expand along logistic growth curves: phases of rapid expansion tend to be succeeded by deceleration when their markets become saturated, or when they have exploited the available potentialities of cost-reducing innovations. European cotton textiles developed along this familiar growth path. After 70 years of impressive growth, by the 1860s the growth rate of the British and other cotton industries decelerated when their potential for further improvements in productivity (through the diffusion of efficient technology and business organisation) diminished. With or without the Civil War world demand for the South's leading cash crop seemed destined to slow up. The cotton boom which had persisted almost unabated from 1802–60 (and which had carried per capita incomes in the old South to within striking distance of Northern standards) was apparently not sustainable. (This thesis has been developed by Wright in [133; 135; 136; 138].)

(iii) THE COSTS AND BENEFITS OF EMANCIPATION

Speculation (in a political vacuum) on how soon and on what terms American slaves might have been emancipated by peaceful agreement seems fruitless. But the immediate and long-term costs of their freedom for the South must surely be included as a key part of any discussion about the costs of war. For slaveowners that point required no argument because defeat for them meant that as a group they lost a property right worth some $2.7 billion (measured in dollars of 1860). (For capital value of slaves see [48, *74*; 92, *53*].) Before the war Southerners had expropriated up to half of the output produced by slaves, and this form of exploitation accounted for proportions of total white income which varied from 31 per cent in the Deep South to 17 per cent in Virginia [94, *224–5*; 55, *261*]. Although the direct loss from emancipation in 1866 affected not more than 40 per cent of all white families resident in the region it imposed a far greater burden on vanquished property owners (apart from the slave revolt in Haiti) than the outcome of any conflict fought before Communist revolutionaries seized power in the wake of world wars in the twentieth century [130, *29*; 131, *95–108*]. And the 'multiplier effects' generated by reduced expenditures of slaveholders spread the effects of abolition among a majority of white Southerners, and to some extent among Northerners as well [94, *226*].

Not all whites suffered. Wage-earners gained something from the removal of competition from cheap slave labour [50, *28–34*]. And (this point requires emphasis) the redistribution of a property right was not equivalent to a real 'loss' for the economy of the South. Emancipation simply accorded slaves legal rights to the full fruits of their own labour. Since their skills and abilities for work remained unimpaired that represented a massive transfer of income from slaveowners to freed men and not a diminution in capacity to produce output for the region as a whole.

Nevertheless the transfer by Federal Law of potential earning power to ex-slaves does not imply that the black workforce of the post-bellum era continued to generate real income for themselves (and the South) in the same way or at the same level as they had done under slavery. After emancipation, agricultural production by freed blacks fell significantly below measured pre-war levels because a majority of blacks exercised their new-found independence and disdained work offered for wages in labour gangs on the old estates [128, *320–6*; 105, *557–75*]. Their refusal to 'work like slaves' led directly to the demise of the plantation system of the ante-bellum South which before the war had successfully produced and exported ever-increasing volumes of cotton, sugar, tobacco and rice [123, *973–6*; 61, *44–5*; 74, *17–20*]. In addition freed black workers opted for more leisure and a much shorter working year than they had been allowed under slavery.

Recent research has just about overturned traditional views that large-scale plantations utilising slaves were less efficient at converting inputs into agricultural output than farms employing free labour. Although the precise scale of the differential and its origins, as well as the methods used to estimate that gap in efficiency, are still in dispute, Fogel and Engerman currently argue that plantations 'were at least 33 per cent more efficient than small farms of the South, slave and free'. (This dispute can be read in [18, *202–3*; 3, *206–26*; 40, *290*; 41, *672–90*].) In their view plantations owed whatever advantages that form of organisation possessed, to economies of larger scale cultivation; in particular to 'the organization of the labour force into highly co-ordinated and precisely functioning gangs characterized by intensity of effort'. Slave gangs exploited economies associated with a refined division of labour, with specific tasks allocated to each worker according to his or her age, skill and physical capacities. The old plantocracy had managed to 'extract' heavy work loads from slaves under various combinations of coercion and incentives. For example their size, together with the diversity of resources at their disposal, allowed plantations to exploit complementarities in the cultivation of different crops. Management saw to it that land, labour and capital were rarely underemployed [40, *290–2*; 80, *147–8*].

After emancipation the refusal of free black labour to work for wages under comparable working conditions led (after a brief interval of experimentation) to the break up of plantation agriculture throughout the South. (The transition period is described in [74, *17–18*; 21, *4–9*; 119, *44–71*].) Although land ownership remained concentrated, management and other productive inputs from the plantations were dispersed (along with former slaves) among thousands of small farms. For freed blacks this represented a tremendous gain in the form of more civilised and autonomous working conditions. But as conventionally measured, agricultural production declined simply because the small-scale farms and the new institutional arrangements for the cultivation of crops proved to be less efficient than plantations. The collapse of the plantation system in the wake of Civil War led to a fall in agricultural output.

That 'loss' which shows up as part of the widening disparity between Northern and Southern income per capita must, however, be offset by the gain in leisure and in job satisfaction enjoyed by millions of ex-slaves, who asserted their right to be treated as whites when they refused to work in gangs or to labour for more than their own preferred number of hours per year [119, *70–1, 131–2*; 21, *4–5*; 93, *58–60*]. Since they withdrew from full-time participation in the labour force black women and their children apparently benefited most from that particular freedom of choice. Blacks suffered no decline in income from this marked improvement in their conditions of work. In 1859 a typical slave consumed about $29 of food, clothing and other necessities (90, *4–7*; 94, *223*]. Twenty years later the income of a black tenant farmer amounted to $42 and after 1879 black per capita incomes rose at a rate which was close to or even above the national average pace of advance (97, *227–8*]. (For a more optimistic view of the growth of black incomes see [61, *97–103*].) But for the Southern economy the 'cost' of emancipation was equivalent to a reduction in measured farm output below historical levels, which had been achieved by forcing its black workers to labour far more intensively and for longer hours than they preferred.

To quantify even roughly the effects of the withdrawal of black labour time from Southern agriculture is not simple. That calculation involves a comparison of the hours black men, women and children had been compelled to work before the Civil War with the hours they chose to work when they became free. It is difficult to estimate hours worked by female and child labour in both slave and post-slave agriculture. But according to Ransom and Sutch 'the effect of freedom was dramatic. The number of man hours per capita supplied by the rural black population fell by an amount between 28 and 37 per cent of the quantity of labour that had been extracted through the coercion of slavery' [90, *13*; 92, *appdx 3*]. That percentage is not accepted by Claudia Goldin whose calculations lump together the decrease in hours worked with the reduction in effort achieved by gang systems on plantations [52, *10–12*]. Furthermore, the withdrawal of black labour reduced farm output only in proportion to its importance as a factor of production. Over time that magnitude depended on how far land, animals and capital were substituted for labour in the cultivation of

crops. In turn that rested upon the supplies of cultivable la
capital and workstock available to a region suffering from t.
devastation of war.

Ransom and Sutch recognise that the Union and Confederate armies had destroyed farm buildings, fences and equipment, decimated livestock and that 20 per cent of the 'improved acreage' of the South went out of cultivation during the 1860s. Indeed, tales of devastation (exemplified by Sherman's rampage through Georgia) are graphic testimony to the immediate impact of warfare. They are *not* inclined, however, to attribute significant long-term effects on output to the destruction of farm inputs. Land, they observe, cannot be permanently damaged by military action. Farm and social overhead capital (particularly railways) seem to have been repaired and replaced rapidly after 1865. Although the livestock population took decades to replenish, the sharp reduction in labour supplies available for the cultivation of crops meant that no overall shortage of mules and horses emerged to reduce the productivity of farmers. In fact, the prices of mules declined relative to their ante-bellum levels. New economic evidence contradicts the 'myth of a prostrate South' and its corollary that the recovery of its agriculture was significantly and for long impeded by shortages of land, capital and workstock, damaged or destroyed by military action. Of course, while battles raged the economic impact of the war was serious. But the diminished capacity of the South for recovery, let alone for sustained growth at the rates the region had witnessed over the first six decades of the nineteenth century must, it seems, be attributable to the demise of slavery and collapse of plantation agriculture [90, *14–22*]. (Again see Goldin's disagreement [52, *10–16*].)

(iv) RECONSTRUCTION AND THE FLAWED TENEURIAL INSTITUTIONS OF THE POST-BELLUM SOUTH

Does modern debate on the effects of Civil War and Emancipation thus end with a grudging recognition that slavery and the plantation system were effective institutions for extracting optimal work loads from a largely unskilled and illiterate black workforce and that the destruction of this inhumane system by military force led to a marked reduction in the capacity of the South to produce agricultural output? Not entirely and because American historians now insist in carrying the argument forward in time so as to evaluate the policies (pursued by the Federal government) for the reconstruction of the Southern economy after the war. In particular, they have been concerned to analyse the new institutional arrangements for agricultural production which emerged upon fertile lands formerly cultivated by black slaves.

Once fighting had ceased several options theoretically existed for re-engaging freedmen and idle plantation land in the business of cultivating food and cash crops in the South. The solution which eventually prevailed came about piecemeal. In the first instance it simply came about as an immediate response to hostility of emancipated slaves (backed by the Freedman's Bureau and other Federal Authorities in the South) to determined attempts by large landowners of the Confederacy to revive their plantations on the basis of contract (and coerced) wage labour [21, *4–10, 189, 192–5*; 119, *119, 132*; 82, *10–13*; 61, *45*]. Planters considered blacks incapable of farming efficiently except in gangs under close supervision. To ensure stability and minimise the turnover of nominally free workers, they persuaded State legislatures to enact codes which seriously impeded the mobility of freedmen [119, *44–7*; 123, *973–6*; 100, *116–17, 137–41, 151–5*]. But their efforts immediately after the war to reconstitute work gangs and to restrict the mobility of black contract labour failed [21, *189–95*; 93, *56–7*; 74, *17–18*].

Secondly, the rapid spread of sharecropping contracts for the cultivation of plantation land (the solution which commended itself as an acceptable compromise to both white landowners and black labourers) also emerged by default because the Federal government did not expropriate and transfer cultivable land along with their freedom to former slaves [74, *16–17*; 119, *116*]. This default has been represented both as a failure of will and imagination on the one hand and, on the other, as a realistic assessment by Conservative Republicans that they lacked a mandate, the power or the resources effectively to distribute the private property of vanquished Southern landowners among former slaves [7, *108–10*; 14, *158–75*; 84, *xi–xiv*].

Apart from a minority of radicals, no politicians in Washington advocated confiscation and wholesale redistribution of plantation land [7, *109–11*; 78, *246–59*; 42, *128–49*]. Lincoln gave the matter little attention and his successor, President Andrew Johnson, undermined even the modest programme for redistribution put forward by the Freedman's Land Bureau [14, *9–10, 178*; 84, *31, 189*; 128, *331*]. Equally, actions sanctioned by Congress in 1861 for dealing with abandoned plantations, the *ad hoc* resettlement policies pursued by General Sherman and other Union commanders on the spot, as well as the reference to 40 acres and a mule in the Freedman's Bureau Bill of March 1865, convinced large numbers of emancipated blacks that the Federal government would somehow provide them with farms as well as with freedom. (See Dubois in [108, *434–5*]; McPherson in [108, *132–55*]; [84, *6–7, 181–2*].)

Alas (and however the issue presents itself in the light of history) at the time Northern politicians from the President downwards failed to see that their endeavours to secure political rights for freedom would be nullified once Federal troops left the South [101, *4–5*; 7, *107–8*]. Yet land reform was not on the cards because most politicians (and probably a majority of the American electorate) did not wish to bring about fundamental changes in property rights in the South. Once the fighting stopped their basic concerns were with reconciliation, with the restoration of a fractured and still fragile Federal Union, and the reduction in military expenditures [101, *14–18*; 84, *31, 196–7*; 14, *159, 162*]. To have created viable family farms for some 4 million ex-slaves would have involved not only a large-scale redistribution of plantation land but massive injections of capital and a defence of black property by Federal troops against revanchiste white Southerners [101, *131*; 14, *165–9*]. The United States offered nothing but freedom to compete in the market place to property-less white immigrants and in 1865 very large numbers of landless whites also resided in the South. In retrospect, and whatever the case in natural justice, land redistribution does not appear as a viable political objective for a democratic government which had just fought a bloody and costly civil war to pursue [131, *95–113*].

Yet the notion is worth exploring because it underlines the failure of the North's political programme to reconstruct Southern society in order to guarantee civil rights for its black population. Furthermore, land redistribution may have constituted a more efficient policy for the reconstitution of Southern

31

agriculture. And that counterfactual seems to be implicit in recent critiques of the post-bellum tenure system by economic historians who have condemned the contractual arrangements which replaced the plantation system on two counts: first on the grounds that sharecropping failed to protect the black population of the defeated Confederacy from economic discrimination, exploitation and coercion by white property owners; and secondly that racism and other flaws embodied in the agrarian institutions of the South operated to depress and restrain the region's capacity for recovery and long-term development [13, 13–30; 127, 523–54; 92, 1–2]. According to this controversial view (ably expounded by Ransom and Sutch) the post-bellum South lacked neither the capital, the labour nor the leadership required to sustain higher rates of growth. But at the end of the Civil War the Federal government (for whatever reasons) did not reform the region's system of property rights and institutions for the allocation of productive resources and this deprived emancipated blacks (and landless whites) of access to cultivable land, workstock, implements, public services, agricultural credit and other inputs on terms that would have augmented their productivity and incomes as well as their social and political status [128, 331; 25, 202–4; 89, 138–46; 92, 82–3; 98, 110].

Instead of a land settlement designed to propitiate black Americans and to promote the long-run growth of Southern agriculture, what emerged on the plantation lands of the former Confederacy was a 'second best' tenure system which, nevertheless, offered an immediate and functional solution to the presence of a large proletariat of black (but also poor white) labourers without land. These families had no ready access to credit or to the means of acquiring even rudimentary skills in farm management. They also remained for the most part immobilised within the South. Numerous local and particular bargains were struck between legally 'free' labourers on the one side, and white property owners on the other. The latter owned not only land but other indispensable means to carry on commercial agriculture such as implements, animals, seed, provisions and credit. Out of the process of negotiation and experimentation there emerged a variety of contractual agreements which constituted the post-bellum arrangements for the cultivation of the old plantations [99, 39–43; 61, 65–7; 92, 82–105; 119, 125–7; 138, 89–98]. That tenure system (complex in the details of its day-to-day working rules) exhibited features which distinguished it from other regions of the United States. Thus, in 1880 and outside the South, four out of five farms were cultivated by their owners compared with only three out of five in the South. Although owner-occupation was in decline throughout the United States, by 1910 contrasts between North and South in the extent of tenancy had become even more pronounced [99, *40*; 85, *1028–32*].

For example, the leasing arrangements which developed in the South were dominated to an overwhelming extent by sharecropping and share tenancy agreements which were more or less freely negotiated in the market place between the owners of land and capital on the one side and landless labourers, black and white, on the other. (The evolution from gang labour through squads to the sharecropping system of family labour after the war is analysed in [138, *90–1*; 99, *41–6*; 61, *66–9*; 127, *526–8*].) Clearly the landless had signalled their preference for sharecropping compared to labouring for fixed daily wages under conditions reminiscent of the discredited slave gang system. Nevertheless in bargains negotiated between rich and politically powerful proprietors and landless blacks and whites, conflicts of interest emerged which revolved around the size of the holding (and its complementary stock of capital) as well as the share of output transferred to property owners for the use of land and other productive inputs. In general terms landowners sought to maximise yields per acre but cultivators wanted to maximise output per family worker and sought large holdings fully capitalised. Landowners' interests led them to offer smaller under-capitalised units upon which the sharecropper and his family would be compelled to labour intensively in order to maximise production and pay the highest rates of return for the land and capital they hired. Landowners' wishes generally prevailed and out of the old plantations they created a new sector of small-scale farms [92, *81–105*; 136, *160–4*; 98, *111–13*]. Such a subsector of agriculture had existed before the war but between 1865–1910 it extended its boundaries to employ the majority of emancipated slaves and their children, together with 35 to 40 per cent of the Southern whites. Thus by 1910, 70 per cent of black and 40 per cent of white Southern farmers were tenants of one kind and another [60, *149–51*]. They farmed but a small percentage of the region's cultivated acreage and gained access to only a limited share of its stock of agrarian capital. Most land and productive capital remained under the control of a minority of white ex-slave owners or was concentrated among larger scale and owner-occupied farms [122, *4–34*; 32, *12*].

That the tenurial system which replaced slavery on plantations gave blacks some autonomy, rewarded enterprise and provided limited possibilites for upward mobility should not be denied. Some blacks gravitated from sharecroppers to tenants, paying cash rents, and an even smaller minority rose into the ranks of tiny landowners. (Higgs, Reid and Alston are concerned to make these points: see [60; 61; 62; 98; 99; 2].) Nevertheless the smallholdings carved out of the old plantations (which may have optimised employment for the region and maximised profits for the minority who leased their assets to landless blacks and whites) also operated to restrain the development of larger and more capital-intensive farms. Only that progression (or migration to Northern cities) could eventually lift the incomes of this largely black proletariat above the lowest rungs of the American ladder. Wright's latest book argues that the economic prospects for blacks who remained in the post-bellum South were severely constrained. The implication of his research is that by providing a majority of blacks and propertyless whites with an acceptable standard of living and tolerable working conditions, sharecropping effectively reduced pressures to migrate North. This institution was in its way as effective as slavery in preventing the absorption and integration of Southern workers into the mainstream of the American labour market [93, *64–6*; 138, *ch. iv*].

Another disadvantage of sharecropping was that it catered for the natural desires of the young to marry early and to cultivate their own holdings with family labour. Under-capitalised farms gave them every incentive to maintain fertility [136, *163–4, 176– 80*; 61, *15*] Before the spread of bollweevil at the end of the nineteenth century, cotton prices and yields remained high enough to sustain poor families on the land. Despite relatively high rates of population increase, push factors seem to have been too weak and pull factors not powerful enough to prompt much outmigration. In any case the majority of unskilled jobs in Northern cities were taken by immigrants from Southern Europe. Blacks were 'crowded out' and Southern agriculture held on to its labour force until the absolute decline in numbers became visible after 1900 [74, *22–3, 74–5*; 32, *208*; 138, *64–80*]. Population pressure within the region which maintained demand for smallholdings also operated to lower the land–labour ratio for black farmers. For example, in 1860 the cultivable acreage of land per black slave amounted to 9 acres. Twenty years later black tenants farmed only 3.0 acres per head [136, *94*]. Labour intensity had clearly increased and leaving things to the market reduced the area of cultivable land available to black farmers. With an elastic supply of cheap labour immobilised in their region, Southern proprietors found it profitable to substitute labour for land as well as for workstock and other inputs in the cultivation of cash and food crops.

Ransom and Sutch add that the post-bellum tenure system also embodied racist preoccupations to maintain blacks at the bottom of the income ladder, to restrict black 'mobility', and to maintain firm control over an ostensibly free labour force. Certainly they cite good evidence where whites either appeared unwilling or found it inexpedient to sell land to blacks [89, *131–9*; 92, *179–81*]. But from the variegated and complex set of contracts for the hire of land and other property available as evidence, it may be impossible to devise acceptable tests for widespread discrimination on grounds of race. (This conclusion seems to emerge from the prolonged debate between Ransom and Sutch [94, *228–33*] and their critics [25, *182–206*; 60, *151–69*; 61; 62; 63].) Legal and other impediments to black mobility certainly existed and implied that some degree of coercion entered into sharecropping contracts [82, *18–28*; 119, *201–3*; 74, *15–16, 20–3*; 122, *66–71*; 123, *981–3*]. How far restraints on mobility depressed the incomes of black farmers below *competitive* levels is difficult to gauge. Higgs is inclined to see the market for tenants as competitive and Wright emphasises the considerable labour mobility which occurred *within* the South – even among sharecroppers. De Canio believes his estimation of a production function (which indicates that sharecroppers received 'competitive' returns) for their labours disposes of the issue [61, *61, 93*; 23, *17–25, 51–70, 120–32*; 138, *64–70, 94–8*]. Furthermore several historians have defended sharecropping on the grounds that the system had advantages for poor blacks or propertyless whites in search of some degree of independence and rewards for personal effort. They argue that this particular form of tenure also shared the risk of crop variance

35

between owners and farmers. 'Reliable' (i.e. deferential) share-croppers and their families could depend on being sustained when harvests fell below subsistence levels. The preferred alternative of fixed rent contracts, which provided farmers with greater opportunities for initiative and recompense for their efforts in increasing output above an agreed cash rent, left farmers to carry the burden of fluctuation in yields [99, *43–6*; 98, *109–27*; 21, *188–9*].

Owners obviously liked contracts which gave them closer control over their land, animals and equipment. No doubt many revelled in the continuation of a power relationship over blacks that was sustained by sharecropping [93, *67*; 74, *30–3, 46–7*]. Indeed some of these agreements reduced tenants' initiatives to a point where their status approximated to that of hired labour [128, *319–34*]. But Higgs has analysed data for 1910 which indicate that a greater proportion of black than white tenants farmed land for fixed cash rents. Although his research refutes crude assertions that race alone determined the type of contract available for access to land, the evidence is also consistent with the hypothesis that white landowners consistently failed to recognise the potential of their black tenants for more independent control over more land and other agricultural resources. Compared to whites cultivating under comparable types of tenure blacks managed smaller and less capitalised farms [60, *149–51*; 132, *171–6*; 138, *99–107*].

Does this observation reflect white prejudice or a prudent assessment of the capacities of their tenants? Economic historians of strict neo-classical persuasion are inclined towards the view that in bargains between white property owners and black farmers the former would rarely be inclined to lease assets on terms that reduced potential rates of return. In other words, as and when it became profitable to enlarge the size of holdings, increase the input of capital and to alter the form of contract for the hire of farms to blacks, then a majority of white property owners would not be prepared to pay a price for discrimination. Market forces would prevail over racial prejudice. (This is the position taken by Higgs [61], Reid [99] and DeCanio [23].) Ransom and Sutch disagree, and expect pervasive and manifest racism among Southerners to distort their perceptions of what might be profitable [89, *134–9*]. Wright observed that the very variety and complexity of contractual arrangements for the hire of land and capital facilitated discrimination on grounds of race as well as personal efficiency (136, *101–3*]. Furthermore, by deliberately obstructing the access of blacks to free education and by close supervision of their farms, whites held back the accumulation of agricultural expertise among a population of largely illiterate ex-slaves [56, *482*; 128, *330–2*; 70, *169–84*; 129, *217*; 76, *9–10*]. For their part, confronted with serious difficulties in acquiring skills (on and off the job) and also by competition from European immigrants for unskilled jobs in Northern cities, blacks seem to have acquiesced in the place open to them within the agrarian system of the reconstructed South and suppressed whatever ambitions they possessed to climb the agrarian ladder. As Higgs so eloquently observed: 'To remain poor, agreeable, and obsequious was after all a form of life insurance [61, *125*]. Their situation was in any case a big step up from slavery.

(v) DEBT PEONAGE AND AGRICULTURAL CREDIT

Just how much human potential was wasted (and output sacrificed) through sharecropping and the pervasive effects of racism and coercion on the land and labour markets of the South seems impossible to measure. The whole structure of small under-capitalised farms (worked either by black or white tenants) operated to constrain capital formation, diversification and moves towards a structure of larger farms within Southern agriculture. For example, poor farmers found it difficult to save and expensive to borrow in order to purchase the implements, draught animals, fertilisers and other inputs required to grow crops more productively. Their access to loans and advances was inevitably restricted by the collateral they could offer and their difficulties were compounded by the collapse and ruin of the old South's reasonably efficient network of credit institutions – dominated by cotton factors linked to large-scale chartered banks [88, *643–51*]. Although banks did reopen after the war and increased rapidly in numbers, by then their services to agriculture had been legally curtailed by Federal legislation which restricted loans or mortgages on real estate and had placed a tax of 10 per cent *ad valorem* on the note issues of state chartered banks [66, *27–30*]. For several decades after the war the South failed to develop a banking system commensurate with its population and widespread demand for agricultural credit. Reasons are not hard to find. Banks tended to locate in towns and in 1880 only a tenth of the population of the South resided in urban centres of more than 2500 people. A majority of potential clients remained illiterate and bankers do not normally deal with customers who cannot readily comprehend their formal bureaucratic procedures. With its incomes, wealth and educational attainment well below the national average, perhaps the South obtained the banks it 'warranted' [9, 862–5]. Nevertheless, they were rather inaccessible and failed to meet the demand for loans required to carry small farmers over the months from sowing to harvest, which left much of the task of supplying credit to shopkeepers or merchants.

In marked contrast to banks, up-country stores (found all over the rural South) appear to have been well located and ready to satisfy demands for ready cash to carry farm families through the seasons and also offered loans for investments undertaken by small farmers. Through a process of continuous dealing and negotiation Southern storekeepers built up information on the capacities of local farmers to borrow, utilise and repay their debts with interest. In agrarian conditions where the available collateral for credit consisted of cash crops (often a single cash crop–cotton) subject to the uncertainties of harvest, and fluctuations in international demand, that process of trial and error could be costly. Indeed, bankruptcy seems to have been endemic among retailers operating on too small a scale for safety, offering funds on the security of a single crop and dealing with a clientele of illiterate, semi-skilled black and white farmers. Storekeepers, furnishing domestic supplies and agricultural inputs on credit, once again represented the immediate and functional response to the emancipation of slaves and the break up of plantations after the Civil War [99, 50–2; 25, 455–7].

Unfortunately, from their standpoint, farmers procured credit essential to carry on commercial agriculture at exorbitant prices. Personal and highly localised contact, together with detailed surveillance which constituted preconditions for access to loans of any kind, provided storekeepers with opportunities to charge 'extortionate' rates of interest [138, 96–7; 92, 126–46; 88, 651–5; 119, 161, 165, 168–71, 172–92]. 'Extortionate' is an emotive adjective and Southern merchants find their defenders among economic historians who claim that farmers *could* 'shop around' among stores in their localities for more advantageous terms, that the South was short of loanable funds, and that the rates of interest charged (estimated at close to 60 per cent a year) represented a more or less competitive price, commensurate with the transaction costs and risks involved for that particular line of business [61, 57–9; 52, 17–24; 99, 50–2; 25, 455–7].

However, Ransom and Sutch insist on categorising the relationship between merchants and small farmers which emerged after the Civil War as one 'debt peonage' [88, 641–65; 58, 159–65]. In their view that relationship (together with the monopoly of legal and political power which the Federal government left in the hands of affluent whites) placed a majority of black (and poor white) farm operators in a situation where they could be exploited. They continue to argue that the mark-ups for supplies purchased on credit cannot be justified by transaction costs, by payments for technical advice, or in terms of the *post-hoc* rate of default [92, 149–68; 95, 66–86; 82, 85–9; 21, 194–5]. (But see [115, 56–63] and for strong disagreement [34, 187–8].)

(vi) THE POST-WAR SUPPLY OF COTTON

Apart from these 'excessively' high payments of interest to merchants (and rents to landowners) the agrarian institutions of the reconstructed South have also been charged with promoting the 'overproduction' of cotton. That particular indictment (prosecuted by Wright) has stimulated more vehement pleas for the defence than other attacks on Southern institutions reconstructed at the end of the Civil War – perhaps because it so clearly embodies a critique of free markets and their avowed tendency to work for the general good of all Americans [136, 164–76; 92, 149–71]. Certain facts are not in dispute. For example, after the war the South became steadily less self-sufficient in the production of food. Food output per capita declined and the region became more specialised in producing cotton. Such trends in the crop mix can be accounted for in terms of the advantages the South undoubtedly possessed in the cultivation of cotton. The theory of comparative advantage would sustain the view that it paid to export more cotton and import more grain and meat, particularly when food prices declined as a result of cheaper transport and the development of Western agriculture [136, *164–76*; 99, *46–8*; 43, *5–23*]. But that same tendency towards specialisation can also be associated with 'flawed' tenurial and credit institutions of the reconstructed South. As a consequence of the Civil War, slave plantations broke up into small tenant farms. Farmers, particularly sharecroppers, were less than sovereign over their choice of crops. And although landowners and their tenants might seem to share a common interest in maximising total revenue from the resources of land, of capital and labour nominally under their joint control, landlords' desires for rent could conflict with the farmers' preference for less work. Their powers could also over-ride the latters' antipathy to risks associated with commercial farming and a commonplace desire for security, which sustained peasant agriculture throughout the world over the nineteenth century [136, *92–3*; 134, *528–44*; 138, *107–14*]. (This desire for security appeared in other agricultural systems in the wake of emancipation – see [32, *191–220*].) Landowners could afford to take risks. They had no interest in peasant-preferences for safety first. Their pressures would be directed towards the cultivation of cash crops and throughout the South smaller tenant farms definitely devoted higher proportions of their tilled acreage to cotton than did the larger and owner-occupied farms [136, *164–76*; 134, *536–44*; 91, *405–25*].

Nevertheless given that small tenants also evinced similar desires to their landlords for profits and that they also appear as responsive as farmers elsewhere in America to changes in relative prices, did specialisation on cotton reduce their incomes below the level that they might have reached with an alternative crop mix containing lower proportions of cotton and higher proportions of food? [22, *608–33*; 23, *ch.7*; 99, *47–9*] Wright (and also Ransom and Sutch) have made the disputed case that specialisation upon cotton (which at first sight appears more profitable than the cultivation of food crops) operated to diminish the incomes of small farmers and did so in direct proportion to their dependence on local storekeepers for supplies of food. Food not grown on the farm or purchased with cash (earned from the sale of cotton) could only be procured on credit afforded by merchants at those 'exorbitant' rates of interest. Cotton cultivation took nearly ten months from seeding to harvest and sale. After they had paid rents and amortised their debts contracted during the previous growing season, farmers rarely retained sufficient cash to cover their family's demands for food, clothing and agricultural inputs required over the year. When harvests fluctuated or whenever prices of cotton declined on world markets their debts accumulated [92, *149–68*; 52, *25–8*]. Ransom and Sutch estimate that a typical black tenant family who purchased food on credit rather than cash in 1879 lowered their real income by 13.5 per cent [95, *81*].

Since a large majority of small farmers were more or less afflicted in this way, why did they not escape from the burdens of debt by growing more food? The answer offered is that 'emancipation from debt' was not possible for small and poor sharecroppers who required cash season after season to service the accumulation of past debt. That alone precluded any substantial reallocation of resources towards food crops. Furthermore, moves towards self-sufficiency in food consumption were resisted by merchants who obtained high profits from furnishing farmers with supplies on credit. They perceived that specialisation on cotton maximised total cash revenue obtainable from each client farm and protected their share of that revenue. Obviously storekeepers looked after their interests by refusing credit on the lien of crops other than cotton. Small tenant farmers, perpetually in need of credit to carry their families and enterprises through the agricultural year, lacked the means to resist (especially if they were black) and grew more cotton than their own sense of security and pecuniary interest demanded [95, *76–86*; 136, *96–9*; 128, *332–4*; 138, *107–14*]. The numbers of farmers afflicted by the crop lien system, the scale of debt burdens carried by farm families, and the precise degree of control exercised by storekeepers on the selection of crops continues to be the subject of dispute. (The sceptics include [115, *56–63*; 52, *17–29*; 22, *609–33*; 23, *94–5, 112–18*; 26, *456*; 61, *56–9*; 34, *187–8*].)

Wright's empirical research not only underpins the view that indebted farmers could have gained by reducing their specialisation on cotton, but he goes on to develop the argument that a cut in cotton exports could have increased the value of total agricultural output for the region as a whole. For several decades before the war, the production of cotton had advanced rapidly in response to British (and European) demand for cotton fibres. After 1860 that demand decelerated from around 5 per cent per annum to 1.3 per cent a year over the period 1866–95. This radical change in world market conditions coincided with the 1860s. With or without the Civil War the long boom experienced by the South before 1860 was not sustainable on the basis of cotton exports. During the wartime blockade cotton output fell drastically and Europe's textile mills found substitutes for American cotton by increasing imports from India, Brazil and Egypt. Prices of higher quality Southern fibres shot up and remained well above their trend level (around 11 cents a pound) over the decade of 'recovery' from 1866–79. During that period the South regained its share of the world cotton market thanks partly to the collapse of Indian supplies during a major famine on that subcontinent, but due basically to the special qualities of Southern fibres. By 1878–9 the world price and American exports had returned to around pre-war levels. Thereafter, cotton output expanded and fluctuated – as it had done for decades before the war – in line with the development of European demand. Unfortunately for the South, the international cotton textile industry had entered a new and far slower phase of its logistic growth curve [136, *89–97*; 135, *630–5*; 134, *526–51*]. (Taking the end year to 1913 cuts the decline to 2.7 per cent a year.)

In these changed international circumstances the 'pressures' towards greater specialisation on cotton exerted by landlords and storekeepers on small tenant farmers turn out to have been unfortunate. Apart from the period of recovery (when Southern producers recaptured markets lost to their Indian, Egyptian and Brazilian rivals during the war) foreign demand was not particularly responsive to reductions in the price of Southern fibres. Wright has estimated the foreign elasticity of demand for American cotton at close to unity, and this implies that the South's total revenue could have been maintained at a constant level by growing less cotton. His econometrics also imply that the land, labour and other resources could have been reallocated to produce food at no extra cost (in terms of reduced export receipts) to the region. Thus if small farmers had been less constrained by the credit system (and by sharecropping) and had been able to follow their own inclinations to produce less cotton and more food, then on this argument the income of the South would have been higher as well as more equally distributed. Such an outcome (which *might* hypothetically have followed from a different land settlement and some alternative and more efficient institutional arrangements for the provision of agrarian credit) would have increased agricultural output. The argument continues to turn on the force of the constraints on the choice of crops exercised by 'flawed institutions' and the area of contention could presumably be narrowed by comparing the behaviour of the small credit-dependent share-croppers with other more fortunate and free farmers of the South. But in no measure could cuts in cotton exports restore conditions for rapid growth experienced by the region over those golden decades before the Civil War. Those conditions were largely exogeneous to the American economy [136, *91–101*] (But see Wright's debate with McGuire and Higgs [77, *69–82*] and [135, *183–95*].)

5 Civil War, Emancipation and the Southern Economy: Some Conclusions

It is time to connect circuits and see if there is any force behind a counterfactual scenario which assumes that without Civil War the Southern economy may have grown at a constant rate. Clearly the short- and long-term penalties of secession from the Union turned out to be grave for the Confederacy (particularly for the Deep South). But just how much of the observed gap between hypothetical and actual consumption per head (Table 4) can be attributed to war as such will remain debatable. It all depends on how the 'effects' of war are defined. Definitions which embrace the break up of plantation agriculture, the reduction in labour time supplied by emancipated blacks, and losses imputable to the agrarian institutions which replaced slavery are bound to suggest far larger effects than definitions which circumscribe the impact of war to include only those costs contingent upon mobilisation and damage to life, limb and property by military action. There is, however, no correct definition and Engerman's point that slavery would have been replaced by a less efficient but more liberal set of agrarian institutions sometime before the end of the nineteenth century is well taken [32, *191–5*]. Thus the numbers in Table 4 represent nothing more than tenable 'outer-bound' estimates of the impact of the Civil War defined to include the full range of effects which followed from hostilities and the subsequent collapse of slavery.

American historians are still engaged in controversies about the efficiency of the plantations of the old South and the inefficiencies associated with the flawed institutions of the reconstructed South. 'Losses' of potential output which can be imputed to the demise of plantations and their replacement by small farms supervised by a hierarchy of landowners and merchants but managed by black tenants are difficult to estimate, particularly when disagreement over 'numbers' extends all the way from those inclined to describe both the slave system and the agrarian institutions which succeeded it as 'economically efficient', to those who deny the efficiency of slavery and who also discover significant inefficiencies in the flawed tenure system of the post-bellum South. Furthermore, the whole basis of the assertion that the Southern economy would have continued to advance at the pre-war rate has been brought into question by Wright, who has shown how world demand for cotton slowed down quite dramatically after 1860.

Confronted with insoluble disputes over definitions and with problems of measuring the manifold influences which operated on the growth rate of the South after the war, historians may feel tempted to give up on the task of reaching any settled conclusions on the economic effects of the Civil War and Emancipation. Goldin and Lewis have, however, given a quantified new focus to the discussion by attempting to separate and weight the three major factors behind the long-term retardation of the South [51, *487– 92*]. Details of their calculations will surely be questioned and revised [113, *900–4*; 114, *493*]. But their methods provide us with the information required to distinguish effects flowing from military conflict from the longer term consequences of emancipation and deceleration in the growth of foreign demand for cotton.

Their first task was to estimate the potential significance of changes in international demand for the region's major cash crop, cotton, because that at least had limited connections with the war and emancipation. Measurement involved computing a 'hypothetical' value of the South's cotton crop in 1879, a computation which was based on an assumption that world demand for cotton continued to expand at its pre-war rate. That econometric exercise indicated that the actual level of demand in 1879 came to only 45 per cent of its hypothetical value. How much cotton might have been exported and at what price, to accommodate demand counterfactually growing at the pre-war rate, involved further assumptions about possible responses from Southern agriculture to the continuation of the cotton boom. Such responses were theoretically conditioned by the prices offered for cotton on world markets and by possibilities available for shifting resources into its cultivation. In making the assumption that output could have been increased at a roughly constant price for cotton, Goldin and Lewis imply that the hypothetical value of the cotton crop in 1879 would have been maximised and the gap between its predicted and actual values is an outer-bound estimate. Other assumptions about 'potential' supplies of cotton are equally plausible. Although cotton is far and away the most prominent example of a cash crop responding to changes in outside demand, other crops exported from the South have yet to be analysed. The full range of linkages to investment and technical change which inevitably flow from exogeneous changes in demand also need to be incorporated into these estimates. Nevertheless some rough notion of the cost to the South from the slowdown in international demand for cotton is useful for historians trying to 'make sense' of the effects of Civil War and Emancipation. Accuracy will not be possible but the Goldin–Lewis figure of somewhere between $2 and $4 billion could possibly be accepted to 'represent' that particular exogeneous effect.

If we are prepared to set aside unresolved and unmeasured elements of the effects of war and simply list them (see Table 5) then, as debate stands at the moment, the evidence amenable to quantification suggests that, in their explanations for the long-term retardation of the South from 1860 to 1914, historians might be prepared to accord roughly equal weight to the impact of hostilities, to the effects of emancipation, and to forces outside the region which had little connection either with the Civil War or with the legacy of slavery.

Damage and destruction from military action are easy to describe and perhaps the least difficult to measure. Fixed reproducible equipment and buildings used in agriculture, industry and transport seem to have been repaired or replaced fairly rapidly after the end of the hostilities. ([45, *chs 1–5*] details the effects of war on Southern agriculture [90, *3, 20*; 113, *905*; 55, *278–9*; 138, *39–46*].) Falls of 30 to 40 per cent are recorded for the region's populations of horses, mules, cattle, sheep and hogs from 1860–6 and the replenishment of livestock took decades [90, *18*; 107, *97–118*; 136, *100, 164*]. Overall, the real value of the South's capital stock (excluding slaves) declined by over 40 per cent during the 1860s and in per capita terms had still not recovered twenty years later [51, *488*; 107, *101*]. Somewhere between 2 and 5 per cent of the South's potential workforce were killed or incapacitated and the economic 'loss' from this most tragic consequence of military conflict reduced the measured output of the Southern economy by something like 13 per cent over the period 1860–1910 [49, *308, 315–16*; 55, *279*].

By destroying slavery and facilitating the replacement of the plantation system with a set of flawed agrarian institutions, the post-war settlement inflicted more permanent damage on the capacity of the Southern economy to produce food and cash crops. After a bloody Civil War the Federal government of a land abundant continent lacked the means, the will or the wisdom to reform the agrarian institutions of the South along lines which (in theory at least) might have utilised the latent skills and capacities of the region's black (and poor white) labour forces more productively. The teneurial system and credit arrangements which actually evolved out of bargains between poor black and white farmers and the property owners of the post-bellum South have been condemned for facilitating discrimination, criticised for perpetuating inequality between whites and blacks and indicted for restraining growth and diversification in the Southern economy.

The last indictment (the subject of protracted debate) will not be easy to prove. On *a priori* grounds, sharecropping may not provide farmers with sufficient incentives to increase labour inputs and enterprise at the margin because up to half of the rewards for extra effort accrue to landowners. Tenants on short leases usually lack any long-run interest in the fecundity of the soil or in maintaining the farm capital they use in good working order. For their part (and because they could not capture full returns from expenditures upon improving land, farm stock and implements) landowners tended to underinvest in the small farm sector of Southern agriculture. Moreover, many preferred to safeguard their assets by resorting to close supervision which mitigated against the evolution of a more skilled body of farmers. Agricultural income accruing to landowners as rent and to merchants in the form of 'exorbitant' rates of interest for supplies purchased on credit also denuded the capacity of small farmers to save and invest. For the South as a whole, the reconstructed tenure system may have promoted an 'excessive' degree of specialisation on cotton. (This paragraph summarises [92] but the view expressed there of Southern agrarian institutions is disputed in [99; 61; 62]. For judicious meditation see [85].)

At the same time 'high/extortionate' rents and interest payments presumably augmented the funds available to landowners and merchants for more profitable investments outside agriculture. Although it is impossible to study the investment behaviour of

Table 5   Estimates of the Long-run Costs of the Civil War and Emancipation for the South

		$ billion (in 1860 $)
1.	*Military costs*	
	1.1 Military expenditures by Confederate, state and local governments	1.03
	1.2 Destruction of productive capital	1.49
	1.3 Loss of life (258,000 killed)	0.68
	1.4 Wounded (197,000 wounded)	0.26
	1.5 Total military costs	3.46
2.	*Cost of Emancipation and reconstruction*	
	2.1 Measured costs imputable to withdrawal of labour time by ex-slaves	1.96
	2.2 Costs contingent upon the break-up of plantations (scale effects)	1.96
	2.3 Losses imputable to the flawed institutions of the reconstructed South	?
	2.4 Losses from racial discrimination	?
	Total lower bound estimate	
3.	*Exogeneous influences (positive and negative) on the growth of the Southern economy*	
	3.1 Deceleration in the rate of growth of world demand for cotton	2.22–4.17
	3.2 Other adverse changes in external demand for cash crops	?
	3.3 Savings and investment	?
	3.4 Technical progress	?
	3.5 Consumption patterns	?
	Total	?

Note: The table makes no reference to 'positive' influences on the post-bellum economy which emanated from the war and emancipation – such as skills acquired by freed black workers, or the diffusion of technology, or consumption patterns and changed attitudes, etc.
Sources: adapted and calculated from data in [49; 51].

these two rival groups systematically, many historians of the South do not regard the post-bellum plantocracy as agents of economic progress. (There was something of a clash of interests between landowners and merchants over the disposition of the agrarian surplus – see [122, 77–85; 58, 153–204; 92, 346].) According to this view vanquished economies recover rapidly from war if they are handed over to new management. Unfortunately reconstruction left economic power in the hands of former slaveholders who retained traditional antipathies towards towns and manufacturing. Thus diversification towards an industrial and urbanised economy proceeded all too slowly: partly because the South's elite of wealth holders gave that development only attenuated and conditional support and partly because they did not welcome and encourage inflows of capital and entrepreneurial talent from the rest of the United States [122, 154–6, 169–76; 74, 30–1, 68–72; 119, 90–1, 201–2; but see 8, 65–6, 70–95].

Recent research has rendered this perception of Southern industrialisation from 1865–1914 less tenable. First, the old plantocracy did not survive the Civil War without losses of land and personnel and new names appeared among the ranks of large landowners all over the post-bellum South [119, 56, 57, 90–1; 100, 172–3]. Secondly, the sense in which the plantocracy can be defined as an anti-capitalist elite which resisted urbanisation and industrialisation before or after the Civil War needs to be carefully defined and documented. Slaveholders are now presented as an acquisitive, commercial and calculating group of American businessmen. (See Genovese [46, chs 7–9] for the traditional view; Fogel and Engerman [39, 67–78] for the new interpretation. For the role of slaveholders as 'modernisers' see [8, ch. 5].) Industry and towns emerged before the Civil War but on a relatively small scale primarily because the elite of the old South were basically interested in maximising the value of their principal asset (slaves) and less concerned than their counterparts in the North in exploiting other resources under their ownership and control [6, 68–9, 98, 127, 157–63]. But when the emancipation of slaves stripped them of more than half their wealth the plantocracy very quickly concentrated upon maximising returns and capital gains from cultivable land, mineral resources, real estate and industrial property which it retained and accumulated through time [138, 17–34; 137, 166–8]. We do not really know how far the plantocracy diversified its wealth and economic interests after the war, but there would seem to be no reason to suppose that most Southern landowners would pass up profitable opportunities to

invest outside agriculture [8, 65–6, 102–3, 113–15; 119, 108–9].
(Storekeepers certainly diversified – see (58, 188–204].) Neither
did they have any pecuniary interest in opposing the growth of
towns and industry within the South. (But see [122, 169–76,
182–3].)

In any case both towns and industry developed at record rates of
growth: industry at 6 to 7 per cent a year from 1869–1909 and the
number of urban centres in the region multiplied over eight times
from 1860–1910. Furthermore, the South participated actively in
the railway boom of 1865–75. Southern industrialisation which
accelerated after 1880 was based upon the availability of cheap
labour for spinning and weaving cotton, upon local timber for
wood products and accessible supplies of coal and ore for the
development of heavy metallurgy around Birmingham, Alabama
[137, 169–71; 138, 39–50].

By any standards, urbanisation and industrial development
proceeded rapidly after the Civil War, but starting late and
proceeding from a low initial level not nearly rapidly enough to
push real wages and per capita incomes up to Northern levels.
Although the region attracted Northern and English capital,
Southerners seem to have been as enthusiastic as other American
investors to boost urban and industrial development particularly
in textiles [10, 43–51; 130, 118–19; 127–8, 131–4; 138, 39–42;
131; 122, 183–4].

Clearly discrimination against the employment of black labour
occurred in Southern industry, especially in textiles. Blacks were
grossly under-represented in skilled and semi-skilled occupations
but received comparable wages to whites at the lower end of
industrial pay scales. There would seem to be little empirical
support for the argument that racism in the labour market held
back the industrialisation of the South before 1914 [136, 679–80;
138, 68–70, 159–72, 177–94].

As historical understanding of economic growth in the South
from 1865–1913 improves it becomes more difficult to apportion
'large shares' of responsibility for the region's persistent backwardness to war, the plantocracy, racism or the flawed tenurial and
credit institutions which emerged out of post-bellum reconstruction. Sharecropping and the failure of banks to service the credit
requirements of small farmers certainly constrained the growth of
agriculture. Racism, particularly in the spheres of education,

employment and contract enforcement, definitely reduced the prospects of blacks for upward mobility. But while the forces of coercion constrained competition, they did not suppress the power of the market to allocate resources efficiently.

Finally, Wright's research has compelled us to reconsider not only the international constraints on the development of Southern agriculture but also the baneful but very long-term effects of slavery. With or without the Civil War European demand for cotton was destined to slow down after 1860 and possibilities for diversification within Southern agriculture were not strong [102, *362–73*; 137, *177*] Structural change towards an industrial and urban South proceeded rapidly enough but the region's peculiar history meant it began from a lower base and with a heritage of obstacles to modernisation, not present in other parts of the United States. In Wright's view the greatest handicap of all was the region's reservoir of unskilled and cheap labour, which remained for generations, immobilised within the region and more or less disconnected from the national labour market. That particular and most persistent legacy of slavery maintained the economy and society of the South in a conspicuously backward position until well after the Second World War [138, chs *2–3*].

6 The Northern Economy

Did Civil War retard or promote the pace of economic advance in other regions of the United States, loosely referred to as the North? There is evidence that legal and institutional changes contingent upon the defeat of the South may have exercised some stimulus to growth over the long run. But that case is not strong and needs to be modestly expressed because its proponents can no longer claim supplementary support from more traditional views which asserted that wartime expenditures by the Federal government made a significant contribution towards Northern industrialisation. (The historiography of this debate, which is focused on the Beard – Hacker thesis, can be read in [4; 126]. It has been reviewed by Scheiber [106, *396–411*].

On the contrary (and as Cochran pointed out) a majority of key statistical indicators mark out the years 1861–5 as a period of slower growth compared either with the 1850s or with post-bellum decades [126, *74–86*]. Even though heightened military expenditure and wartime procurement might be expected to stimulate more rapid advance in selected sectors of industry (such as engineering, iron, woollens, provisions and shipbuilding), the overall impact of war-related demand on these industries failed to compensate for the loss of markets and dislocations suffered by other sectors of manufacturing. For example, while the woollen industry enjoyed prosperity from governmental orders, cotton textiles slumped for want of raw material. Boots and shoes made in Massachusetts lost markets in the South. Iron utilised to manufacture small arms amounted to only a tiny fraction of iron embodied in the railway lines laid down before the war from 1856–60; and railroad investment declined sharply during the conflict; so did residential construction. Although pig iron production held up, no major industry experienced anything like its post-bellum rate of increase from 1866–80. Apart from woollens and watches, it seems difficult to find any *industry-wide* examples of accelerated growth from 1860–5. Nearly all statistical data point the other way and in the industrialised states of Massachusetts and New York the real value of manufactured output declined by large margins. (See Engerman in [28, *373–4*; 118, *276–7*]. For the older view see [33].)

Furthermore, there seem to be few organisational or technical changes in industry which might be associated directly with the Civil War. Pressure from a gun company led Joseph Brown to develop the universal milling machine in 1862. Military demand prompted McKay's improvement to the machine for stitching soles to the uppers of shoes. In general, though, the war generated few innovations, even in weaponry, and served basically to distract scientists and technologists from the pursuit of more utilitarian objectives [47, *62–8*]. But it may have hastened the diffusion of techniques which were known before conflict erupted.

Outside the South agricultural production grew rapidly in wartime, despite the mobilisation of its manpower to fight for the union. Although rapid advance had commenced earlier, the war certainly imparted some extra stimulus to Northern and Western agriculture. From 1864–6, urban food prices jumped about 70 per cent above pre-war levels. Inflation encouraged farmers to shift more rapidly into commercial agriculture, and wartime labour shortages prompted them to mechanise. Thus the output of farm implements and machinery which increased by 110 per cent from 1849–59, jumped to 140 per cent from 1859–69 and fell to 95 per cent from 1869–79. Capital invested in the manufacture of farm machinery went up by a factor of 3 from 1860–70. Drills, reapers, mowers, threshers and horserakes diffused among farmers in Ohio, Illinois, Michigan and Wisconsin and increased labour productivity by 13 per cent over the 1860s; compared to 8 per cent over the previous decade. Thus labour shortages and inflation, induced by the Civil War, operated to sustain – and to quicken – tendencies towards mechanisation in Northern and Western agriculture. Northern farmers had a good war but presumably the stimulus to growth was minor compared to longer term forces at work, such as the extension of railways, the opening of new lands to the West and Europe's growing demand for imported farm produce [45, *160–1, 170, 187, 232–40, 378–9*; 96, *187–95*].

Federal expenditures to prosecute war failed to compensate industry for the dislocation and interruptions to the economy associated with military mobilisation. Indeed in so far as that expenditure simply substituted for normal civilian consumption of food, clothing, housing and manufactured goods, it is difficult to see how the redistribution of income from taxpayers to government could expand aggregate demand. Any stimulus could only be specific to given sectors, and in the absence of detectable 'spinoffs' was without obvious significance for the long-term growth of industry as a whole, (see Engerman in [28]. A good textbook treatment is by Vatter [117, *37–59*].) If they are to be found, economic benefits for the Northern economy must be traced in the methods used by the Federal government to finance its military programme.

(ii) THE ECONOMIC CONSEQUENCE OF INFLATIONARY FINANCE

Only a small proportion of the extra finance required to prosecute war came from taxation [116, *209–15*; 117, *37–59*]. Like its predecessors in other wars and European governments in the eighteenth century, Lincoln's administration paid its bills for military action against the South with borrowed and printed money. The famous greenbacks and other issues of fiat currency covered 28 per cent of the deficit between expenditure and receipts, short-term liquid assets a further 33 per cent and bonds the remaining 39 per cent. Liquid assets (and to some extent, bonds) were monetised by banks in the form of notes and deposits. Well over 60 per cent of the expenditures not financed by higher taxes were covered by methods that added directly and indirectly to the Union's supplies of money and thereby promoted that familiar phenomenon of wartime inflation [24, *314–17*; 110, *137–61*].

By selling paper securities to banks and using fiat money the Federal government obtained the means to bid goods and services away from its own citizens – in particular from those groups whose money incomes failed to keep pace with the general rise in prices. Inflation which proceeded at 13 per cent a year from 1860–5 was not only the visible symptom of a fiscal process designed to appropriate resources for war; it also operated to transfer income between social groups in ways apparently conducive to the longer term advances of the Northern economy. During the Civil War income was redistributed from those whose remuneration lagged behind rising prices to those whose incomes kept ahead of prices. As long ago as 1903 Mitchell pointed to the pronounced lag of wages behind prices between 1860–5. But his conclusion that this represented a redistribution of income to capitalists in the form of profits has been challenged on the grounds that it was indirect taxes and the higher costs of imported commodities that pushed prices ahead of wages. Inflation redistributed income to the state and to foreign exporters rather than to Northern businessmen [69, *459–67*]. More recently DeCanio and Mokyr re-established Mitchell's insight into the *short-run* effects of the inflation upon Northern workers. Their econometric study suggests that real wages fell by 30 per cent and at least half and probably two-thirds of that decline can be imputed to institutional constraints in the labour market, which prevented wages from moving in line with prices during the war years. Businessmen gained and their employees lost from the inflationary methods utilised by the Federal government to finance the war effort (24, *311–36*].

How they used their 'windfall' profits is difficult to investigate. No doubt some part of the gains from inflation were recycled to the Treasury when businessmen purchased Federal bonds. Apparently manufacturers also utilised profits to redeem their debts and to reduce their dependence on wholesale merchants: which over the long run promoted a less competitive and more concentrated industrial structure [86, *10*, *11*, *116*, *126*]. Some portion was consumed and the rest funded investment to sustain the productive capacity of the Northern economy. The influence of inflation on capital formation in wartime could not have been substantial unless investors gained at the expense of groups other than hired labour. In any case the long-term effects depended on the type of capital created. Inflationary interludes often signal and promote investments in activities that contribute little to development over time. After the war (when price deflation succeeded inflation) real wages rose again and the share of profits in total income presumably declined (Engerman in [28, *375–7*]). Real rather than monetary forces determined the share of wages in American national income over the nineteenth century and there can be no presumption that the wartime inflation shifted the distribution of income from 1866 to 1914 for or against profits, savings and investment.

(iii) FEDERAL DEBT AND PRIVATE CAPITAL FORMATION

To maintain the Union the Federal government borrowed huge sums of money and America's national debt multiplied from about $59 million in 1859 to $2756 million in 1866. On an annual basis loans raised by central (and state) governments were almost equivalent to the share of their incomes saved and invested by citizens of the North in the 1850s [116, *209–11*; 24, *314–17*]. This massive diversion of investible funds from the formation of capital for productive purposes towards the funding of military forces severely constrained possibilities for private investment during the war years and must go a long way towards explaining the poor performance of the economy in the 1860s. Unlike the South, the capital of the North was not damaged by warfare but the Treasury's voracious demand for funds led to the depreciation and to much reduced levels of expenditure on new productive assets.

After the Civil War successive Federal governments pursued a policy of debt retirement. Between 1866–93 America's debt diminished to 35 per cent of its immediate post-war level, as year after year surplus tax revenue was utilised to redeem bonds issued during the war. Given that the diversion of investible funds into Federal debt severely restrained capital formation from 1860–6, to what extent did the transfer of tax revenue towards bond holders for more than two decades after the end of the war operate to promote savings and investment? Federal customs and excise duties financed this reverse flow and seem to have been 'regressive' in their incidence. Thus the policy of debt retirement transferred income from the majority of taxpayers to a richer social group of bondholders, with higher than average propensities to save and invest. Flows of taxes paid as interest on government debt outstanding moved in the same direction. Furthermore, since the state contracted debt at a time of rising prices and redeemed it when prices fell the *real* value of money repaid went up. (Policy is described in [110, *161–92*], see also [112, *ch.5* and *164–75*; 97, *368–70*].)

To discern some positive influence on capital formation from the policy of debt retirement and interest paid to bondholders is a start but to measure longer term effects is extremely difficult and the three estimates now available depend critically on assumptions used to specify responses to debt retirement. For example, Engerman conducted his calculation on the supposition that bondholders saved and invested a far higher proportion of their incomes than taxpayers in general. He assumed 40 per cent more and that percentage provided him with an estimate of the extra savings generated by debt redemption. But his estimate added only one point to the ratio of capital formation to GNP from 1875–84. He concluded only a tiny proportion of post-war growth could be attributed to debt repayment [28, *378*].

Basing his argument on modern theories designed to explain the behaviour of capitalists who hold portfolios of paper assets, Williamson preferred to assume that as the Treasury retired debt, bondholders would replace Federal assets with an identical amount of private securities. Retired debt thus augments private savings by a comparable sum. In addition he supposed that 40 per cent of the flows of interest would be saved. On these assumptions the ratios of investment to national income would be augmented not by one but by three percentage points from 1866–72 and by two percentage points from 1869–78, with correspondingly larger effects on long-term growth [125, *611–36*].

The most recent and sophisticated attempt to measure the impact of debt management on capital formation and growth has been conducted by James in the context of a fully specified model of income determination for the American economy, 1872–1900. His model and econometrics support the view that changes in the volume of public debt influenced levels of private investment but principally through changes in interest rates, rather than by way of direct substitution of business for government securities in private portfolios. In his conclusions James rightly observed that the assessment historians make of post-bellum debt management should logically be predicated on some posited alternative uses of taxes collected from the public, 1866–90. If redemption had been abandoned and the stock of debt held constant then by 1890 America's stock of capital could have been 3 per cent smaller and national income nearly 4 per cent lower. But the Federal government could also exercise other options. Taxes might have been reduced but since the bulk of revenue came from tariffs (strongly supported by protectionist lobbies) lowering tariffs does not appear as a plausible policy for Republican administrations to pursue. Thus if debt had not been retired, revenue might have been deployed to raise government expenditure and changes in that variable could raise the level and growth of national income. James estimated that the combined effect of a policy to hold debt constant and spend surplus tax revenue on something else would be to reduce the capital stock for 1890 by around 6 per cent and to increase national income by nearly 2 per cent [67, *tables 2 and 3*]. *Ex post* debt redemption may have been a good thing: in the sense that modern American economists find it unrealistic to model alternative budgetary policies with more positive effects on development. Nevertheless the overall effect of debt retirement on the growth rates, 1865–1914 seems to have been far too small to compensate the Northern economy for the 'crowding out' of private capital formation which followed from the massive diversion of investible resources to fund the preservation of the Union from 1861–5.

(iv) FEDERAL DEBT AND THE DEVELOPMENT OF THE AMERICAN CAPITAL MARKET

At the core of structural change is capital formation financed by savings. That process will be promoted by a developed network of financial intermediaries (such as banks, trust and mortgage companies, brokers and insurance firms) which will encourage people to save. These firms should in theory allocate the investible funds of their clients more efficiently among competing uses. Financial institutions attract savings by offering a range of securities of differing maturity and risk to potential investors. By their knowledge and skill they promote flows of funds across regions and sectors of an economy for productive purposes and that raises overall rates of return on capital [112, *ch. 4*].

Long before 1860, the institutions of the American capital market had evolved steadily in response to growing demands from agriculture, industry and commerce for loans and credit. During the war, the Federal government appeared on the scene to borrow vast sums of money – equivalent in all to twice the amount invested in ante-bellum railroads. That intense effort to mobilise savings for military purposes was entrusted to a Philadelphia banker, Jay Cooke, who set up a nationwide sales organisation to market Federal securities. His success in providing the government with the indispensable means to prosecute war widened the habit of savings and investing in paper securities among the population at large [97, *347–9*; 112, *ch. 5*].

During the war banks and other intermediaries became actively involved in dealings in government securities. That involvement which operated to integrate or 'nationalise' the market for capital in the United States was reinforced when Congress passed laws in 1863 and 1864 to compel banks (chartered by government and called national banks) to hold stipulated amounts of Federal debt [97, *345–51*]. The connections between banks and the state continued for two decades after the war, during the Treasury's programme of debt redemption. Furthermore, although commercial banks had spread rapidly in the 1850s, continuation of this trend persisted throughout the 1860s, when the numbers of national, state and private banks increased from 2687 to 3776 [66, *25*; 112, *ch. 4*]. Governmental demand for their services and the profits to be made from dealing in public securities surely played some part in that development? For example, the placing of Federal debt provided banks (and other intermediaries) with a relatively secure basis for investment upon which they could diversify towards the riskier assets offered as collateral by private business. In short, management of Federal debt during and after the Civil War improved the efficiency with which the capital market garnered and allocated investible funds. Lessons learned in 'high' finance could then be applied to support the 'mundane' expansion of industry, agriculture and transport after 1865.

At the same time as the marketing of public securities helped to promote mobility of capital, Federal legislation in the form of National Banking Acts, 1863–4, operated to restrain and retard the diffusion of a free enterprise banking network throughout the United States [66, *27–9*; 111, *244–6*]. Those acts and subsequent regulations were a direct outcome of Civil War, in that the Congress of those years aimed to provide all American states with a truly 'national' currency, backed exclusively by the bonds of the Federal government. That kind of legislation (which conveniently extended and guaranteed the market for public securities) would not have passed through the ante-bellum Congress.

In effect, wartime regulations which restricted entry to the business of banking and confined note issues to banks chartered by Federal authority, arrested the development of branch banking and prohibited loans on mortgages [112, *ch. 2*; 117, *52–4*]. Federal law did not apply, however, to banks chartered by state governments who formulated their own codes for the establishment and operation of financial institutions. Although state banks refrained from the issue of notes (which could be taxed at 10 per cent *ad valorem*) they avoided that tax by substituting deposits for notes. In the post-bellum era cheques rapidly superseded bank notes as the major means for making payments. Their use spread rapidly, even into rural areas. Private unincorporated banks also arose in large numbers to meet demands for services which banks regulated by Federal or state governments could not supply [66, *29–44*; 97, *362–5*].

Governmental regulations moulded and restrained but certainly did not arrest the diffusion of banks across America. Prohibitions on branch banking (which *prima facie* may well have reduced the transfer of funds from bank to bank, from region to region and from sector to sector) were likewise circumvented by informal but well-established connections, developed through a system of correspondent banking. Long before the Federal government eventually amended its restrictive legislation in 1900, American enterprise had created something like an integrated national market for the movement of investible funds across a vast territory and from one sphere of economic endeavour to another [66, *chs 4 and 5*; 112, *ch. 3*].

But as differentials in rates of interest and access to bank credit reveal, terms upon which potential investors could borrow in different regions of America varied widely. Allowing for risk and transaction costs, a perfectly functioning network of financial institutions should display strictly limited differentials in local prices charged for loans and credit. Areas or activities exhibiting high rates of interest (and indicating a strong demand for investible resources) would attract loanable funds. At the same time, regions with lower rates of return on productive capital would experience diminished demands for funds and would 'export' savings, through the banking network, for investment in assets promising higher rates of return. Something approximating to this mechanism operated (but imperfectly) in the United

States for nearly four decades after the Civil War [19, *355–9*; 66, *ch. 6*].

Among *several* factors which slowed down the more rapid development of the American capital market towards optimal efficiency was Federal legislation passed at the height of the Civil War. That legislation acted as an obstacle to the development of an integrated and well-functioning structure of financial institutions. By restricting entry the law discouraged competition among banks, particularly in the West and South of the United States. Local banks (and other intermediaries) could be more or less uninhibited in charging their clients widely disparate rates of interest because they operated under limited competitive pressures to maximise returns on the investible funds placed at their disposal [66, *199–210*; 112, *ch. 5*]. James found that the steady erosion of local monopoly powers in financial markets explains a high percentage of the convergence of regional interest rates between 1870 and 1910 [65, *878–97*; 66, *chs. 6 and 7*].

We should, however, conclude this section on banks with Williamson's question: did the legal constraints on the evolution and action of financial intermediaries really matter? Would a competitive, perfectly functioning and integrated market for capital have augmented American growth between 1866 and 1914 by a large percentage? Historians of financial institutions may be inclined to attribute too much significance to the role of intermediaries in raising rates of saving, depressing long-term rates of interest and encouraging investment after the Civil War [125, *144–5*]. Imperfections in the structure and organisation of banking apparently stimulated a net outflow of short-term funds from countryside to the towns, from agriculture to industry and from the capital-short regions of the West and South into relatively safe assets issued in the capital-abundant cities of the North and East. Some part of those seemingly 'perverse' drains of funds returned in the form of long-term loans – as intermediaries in New York, Boston, Philadelphia and other Eastern financial centres recycled funds into equities and mortgages of developing regions [66, *ch. 5*]. Sylla applauded imperfections in the capital market which, he argued, positively encouraged higher rates of industrialisation and urbanisation [112, *ch. 5*], while Williamson's simulation exercises suggest that a perfectly integrated capital market would have made very little difference to savings rates or the growth of per capita income from 1879–1910. He concludes: 'The social savings of a perfect capital market would have been disappointing . . . the asserted beneficial aspects of financial intermediation are even more doubtful' [125, *145*]. Williamson believes that the connections between banking legislation and the integration of the capital market on the one side and the long-term development of the American economy on the other are interesting to analyse but probably of no great significance for the rate of growth.

(v) TARIFFS

One of the enduring consequences of the Civil War was protection-ism against foreign imports into the United States. American tariff history is well-documented and may be summarised as high and rising duties from 1816–32 succeeded by a series of rationalisa-tions and reductions which brought down the average rate on dutiable imports from around 62 per cent *ad valorem* in 1830 to 20 per cent by 1860. Tariffs imposed to finance military expenditure and to offset excises imposed on domestically produced com-modities for the same purpose pushed the rate to nearly 50 per cent in wartime and it remained in the 40 to 50 per cent range for the rest of the century. Politically, victory for the North reversed a tendency towards free trade between 1832 and 1861, which had been strongly supported by the South. Thereafter successive Republican administrations favoured a policy of protection [118, *217–19*; 97, *387–91*].

Unfortunately the familiar nominal rates of duty, expressed *ad valorem*, are an inadequate guide to the advantages enjoyed by industries from tariffs. Such advantages are properly calculated in terms of 'effective protection' which might be defined as the extra net incomes *potentially* available to the owners of the assets and to their employees engaged in particular industries which flowed from the imposition of restraints upon imports. Percentage rates of effective protection answer the question how much *extra* profit and wages *could* an American industry theoretically enjoy as a result of tariffs before the price charged for its products invited foreign competition. One estimate of the average for 21 major industries in 1889 comes to 100 per cent and effective rates were certainly higher from 1866 to 1889 [59, *89–99*]. Tariffs provided American industrialists with opportunities to augment profits and to pay their workers higher wages, not only to the detriment of foreign rivals but at the expense of the real income of their fellow citizens, compelled to consume more expensive domestically produced manufactured goods. Now the gap between prices actually charged by American firms enjoying protection and a 'hypothetical' set of free trade prices has not been calculated and it is not possible to estimate the income transferred from consumers to producers which resulted from the policies of protection, pursued during and after the Civil War. Obviously such transfers would vary from industry to industry and firm to firm. Competitive industries would charge prices for their wares close to world market prices. Only less efficient sectors of American industry required protection and 'exploited' domestic consumers. Against this overall 'loss' of consumer welfare and choice (which is an inevitable concomitant of protection) there can be set 'hypothetical long-term gains' in the form of faster rates of industrialisation and per capita income growth. Republicans and their supporters usually defended the high tariffs, maintained after 1866, with reference to familiar infant industry arguments and rarely hesitated to impute the successful development of particular sectors of manufacturing to the advantages of restraints imposed by their administrations upon foreign competition [64, *403–10*].

Economic historians accept the point that tariffs played *some part* in the establishment of particular American industries in their early phases of development but recent empirical studies are not inclined to accord a large weight to protection in explanations for the growth of such important sections of manufacturing as cotton textiles and iron even in the ante-bellum period. For example, Fogel and Engerman's analysis demonstrates that production of American pig iron expanded rapidly from 1842–58 despite sharp reductions in the tariff and in the price of British imports [38, *155–62*]. Zevin's research on New England textiles suggests tariffs made only a limited contribution to the growth of the cotton industry from 1815–33, because by the end of the war with Britain (1812–14), American firms had already taken over the cheaper end of the domestic market for textiles [139, *125–37*]. Taussig's famous study of tariffs (first published in 1892) which concluded that (apart from cotton spinning and silk), American industrialisation received no significant help from protection is beginning to receive empirical backing from econometric history [16,95–168].

If only agnostic support can be derived for two important examples of infant industries (cotton and iron) and that for the decades before 1860 then any argument that the expansion and widening of the industrial base required the high levels of protection afforded by Republican administrations from 1870–1910 begins to look spurious. America possessed comparative advantages for most forms of industrial activity which developed in that subcontinent after the Civil War. In the absence of detailed industry studies which validate the case for infant industries, it is safer to conclude that tariffs seem neither necessary nor in any way sufficient for the long-run advance of American manufacturing.

To argue industry had little need of tariffs in no way disposes of the more plausible case that the redistributive effects of protection operated to speed up structural change and trends towards higher standards of living. In comparison to an implied counterfactual scenario where nominal tariffs levied on manufactured goods remained at or around their ante-bellum rate of 20 per cent *ad valorem*, the post-war system of protection certainly led to higher profits and wages in the manufacturing sector, which may have attracted more immigrants and foreign capital to the United States. In so far as the urban economy was characterised by higher propensities to save and invest, then by promoting the allocation of income away from agriculture towards industry, Republican policy probably augmented overall rates of saving and investment. Tariffs also altered the structure of relative prices which reinforced that tendency. First, the prices of unprotected farm produce were depressed relative to the prices of protected industrial goods. Furthermore, higher tariff rates tended to be imposed upon finished manufactures and lower or zero rates appeared on intermediate inputs and capital equipment. Construction activity derived few benefits from protection. Thus tariff schedules appear to have been designed to lower costs upon imported producers' equipment, urban construction goods, and other inputs which entered the highly protected manufacturing sector [125, 656–61; 20, ch. 18].

Nevertheless, the positive impact of these influences on the rate and pattern of development exhibited by the American economy after the Civil War has not been quantified. Neither is it at all clear that the departure from short-term comparative advantages and specialisation, promoted by post-bellum tariffs, was the optimal growth path for the American economy from 1865 to 1914. Lower tariffs, even shifts to free trade (at the expense of Northern manufacturing), would have brought short-run benefits, not only to agriculture and to the Southern states but also to the growth of the international economy as a whole. For the United States the adjustment costs associated with more liberal trade could have been rather small [66, *233–53*]. Unless the post-bellum tariff policy succeeded in compelling suppliers to lower their prices to maintain some share of the American market there is no reason to assume that such hypothetical gains from shifts in the terms of trade exceeded the costs which flowed from the allocation of resources into lines of manufacturing where the United States possessed no obvious and immediate advantages. The case for tariffs remains unproven.

7 Civil War and the American Economy: Conclusions

In contrast to the historiography of the South, there is a tradition of describing, indeed of emphasising, the gains the North derived from its victory in 1865. That tradition stems largely from the writings of historians (such as Charles Beard and Louis Hacker) who were disposed to perceive events as tragic as the American Civil War as a 'watershed' or 'turning point' in the economic life of the nation. But so many influences were at work in the economy that all claims made for the beneficient effects of war on the North must be carefully specified, connections with structural change identified and their contribution to the growth rate measured. Above all, historians now insist that a proper economic appraisal of war should be conducted within a framework which compares its costs and benefits with other policy options available at the time. For example, any scheme to compensate white Southerners for the emancipation of slaves would have cost Northern taxpayers far less than war. With hindsight, it is even difficult to conceive how the permanent secession of slave states from the Union might have damaged the economic prospects for the North. Although slaves gained enormously from the Civil War there can be no presumption that the political union which survived a costly attempt to break it up constituted an optimal political unit for a long-run economic progress.

Southerners who supported secession would certainly agree. Trade and other economic connections between the North and an independent Confederacy would almost certainly have survived secession (*pace* Canada in 1783). Northerners looking back when the guns fell silent at the enormous bills they had shouldered to maintain the United States and considering the damage military action and the abrupt abolition of slavery had inflicted on their markets in the South might then have wondered about a better way. As time went on and Federal taxes continued to be collected from citizens of the 'affluent' North to sustain living standards in a 'backward South', any *material* gains from prosecuting a bloody Civil War receded in the perceptions of Americans into the realms of the highly problematical. Until, that is, Charles Beard, Louis Hacker, William Miller and other historians reminded them that the 'Triumph of American Capitalism' owed something (and perhaps a great deal) to the victory of the North. (This historiography has been surveyed and debated by Cochran and by Salsbury in [4, *148–61, 162–9*] and by Scheiber [106, *396–411*].)

Unfortunately, that reminder neglected to set the Civil War in its long-run context and failed to examine and to quantify its costs and benefits in the round. Positive economic effects did flow from the methods utilised by the Federal government to defray its military expenses. Inflationary finance augmented the profits of businessmen as wages lagged behind prices. Not for long and in no measure could windfall profits from inflation make up for the massive diversion of funds away from private investment into army coffers. Government borrowing 'crowded out' private capital formation from 1860–5 but the consistent policy of debt redemption stimulated investment for over two decades after the war. That policy perhaps added up to 2 per cent to national income in 1890 – positive, yes, but hardly compensation for the long-term effects contingent upon the destruction, depreciation and neglect of America's stock of capital for more than five years in the 1860s. Management of the national debt by the Treasury (attended by Federal regulation of national banks) again exercised positive effects on savings and investment and the efficiency of financial intermediaries during and after the war. Yet there seems to be no reason to posit substantial spin offs to growth from the activities of government in the capital market. High tariffs do represent an enduring consequence of the Civil War. There is no evidence, however, that Northern industry required the levels of protection it enjoyed from 1860 to 1914 or that the distributive effects of tariffs really 'jacked up' rates of saving, investment and thereby promoted an allocation of resources which in the long run fostered higher levels of per capita income – even in the Northern states.

Neither North nor South engaged in Civil War to achieve economic gains. Even white Southerners fought merely to defend a valuable property right in slaves. As a result of defeat their region, particularly the Deep South, suffered decades of economic deprivation from destruction wrought by warfare, from the enforced and abrupt abolition of plantation slavery and from the failure of Northern and Southern politicians to reconstruct the political and agrarian institutions of the South on a more efficient basis after the war. And there can be no question that the failure of American democracy to bring about a peaceful transition from a slave to a free labour market in 11 states of the Union imposed substantial losses on the economy of the South for decades after the termination of the Civil War. Slavery could not, it seems, have survived for many decades after 1860 and the costs of its violent and abrupt demise during the Civil War should be considered against alternative and other emancipations carried out elsewhere in the New World. (Woodward [131] and Engerman [32], compare it with other slave emancipations in the Americas.) American historians may also wish to react to the assertion that European states (even Tsarist Russia) probably managed their transitions from feudal to free labour markets more effectively.

Although the costs of secession and civil war fell heavily and disproportionately on the white citizens of the Confederacy, the Unionists also suffered a marked and definite decline in their consumption for nearly two decades after the attack on Fort Sumter. Of course the war enhanced the powers of Northern politicians to enact Federal legislation in the interests of Yankee businessmen. Historians have listed several laws passed during and in the aftermath of the conflict (related to banks, the public domain, tariffs, contract labour, etc.) which ostensibly favoured an 'industrialising' North over an 'agrarian' South as well as measures which favoured Western agriculture [45, 263–5, 377–8]. That dichotomy of interest was never clear cut. Given time and shifts in political power congress may well have enacted somewhat similar legislation with or without the military defeat of the Confederacy. Furthermore, the economic significance of these reforms said to be favourable to the advance of 'industrial capitalism' should not be exaggerated. Even at its height the power of the South cannot be seriously represented as a shackle on the industrial progress of the United States. Similar agnosticism is surely the most reasonable response to other posited economic advantages derived by the North from waging war. On examination they turn out to be a small recompense – a tiny offset towards the huge economic burden borne by generations of Americans to emancipate slaves and to hold the Union together. Freedom is certainly priceless. Politically the Federal Union may have been worth preserving. But in purely material terms the Civil War did not pay.

Bibliography

[1] M. Aldrich, 'Flexible Exchange Rates, Northern Expansion and the Market for Southern Cotton: 1866–79', *Journal of Economic History*, XXXIII (1973), 399–416.

[2] L. S. Alston, 'Tenure Choice in Southern Agriculture 1930–60', *Explorations in Economic History*, 18 (1981), 211–32.

[3] *American Economic Review*, LXIX (1979), 206–26.

[4] R. Andreano (ed.), *The Economic Impact of the American Civil War* (1962) and (1972).

[5] F. Bateman and T. Weiss, 'Comparative Regional Development in Antebellum Manufacturing', *Journal of Economic History*, XXXV (1975), 182–209.

[6] F. Bateman and T. Weiss, *A Deplorable Scarcity* (1981).

[7] H. Belz, 'The New Orthodoxy in Reconstruction Historiography', *Reviews in American History* (March 1973).

[8] D. B. Billings, *Planters and the Making of the New South, 1865–1900* (1979).

[9] W. W. Brown and M. O. Reynolds, 'Debt Peonage Reexamined', *Journal of Economic History*, XXXIII (1973), 862–71.

[10] D. L. Carlton, *Mill and Town in South Carolina, 1880–1920* (1982).

[11] T. Cochran, 'Did the Civil War Retard Industrialization?' in [4].

[12] A. H. Conrad and J. R. Meyer, *The Economics of Slavery* (1964).

[13] L. and J. Cox (eds), *Reconstruction, the Negro and the New South* (1973).

[14] L. Cox, *Lincoln and Black Freedom* (1981).

[15] P. David, 'The Growth of Real Production in the United States Before 1840', *Journal of Economic History*, XXVII (1967), 151–95.

[16] P. David, *Technical Choice, Innovation and Economic Growth* (1975).

[17] P. David *et al.* (eds), *Reckoning with Slavery* (1976).

[18] P. David and P. Temin, 'Slavery the Progressive Institution', in [17].

[19] L. Davis, 'The Investment Market, 1870–1914: The Evolution of a National Market', *Journal of Economic History*, XXV (1965), 355–99.

[20] L. Davis *et al.*, *American Economic Growth* (1971).

[21] R. F. L. Davis, *Good and Faithful Labour* (1982).

[22] S. DeCanio, 'Cotton Overproduction in late Nineteenth Century Southern Agriculture', *Journal of Economic History*, XXXIII (1973), 608–33.

[23] S. DeCanio, *Agriculture in the Post-Bellum South* (1974).

[24] S. DeCanio and J. Mokyr, 'Inflation and Wage Lag During the American Civil War', *Explorations in Economic History*, 14 (1977), 311–36.

[25] S. DeCanio, 'Accumulation and Discrimination in the Post-Bellum South', *Explorations in Economic History*, 16 (1979), 182–206.

[26] S. DeCanio, 'Review of One Kind of Freedom', *Economic History Review*, XXXII (1979a), 455–7.

[27] R. A. Easterlin, 'Regional Income Trends', in S. E. Harris (ed.), *American Economic History* (1961).

[28] S. L. Engerman, 'The Economic Impact of the Civil War' in R. W. Fogel and S. L. Engerman (eds), *The Reinterpretation of American Economic History* (1971).

[29] S. L. Engerman, 'A Reconsideration of Southern Economic Growth, 1770–1860', *Agricultural History*, XLIX (1975), 343–61.

[30] S. L. Engerman and E. Genovese (eds), *Race and Slavery in the Western Hemisphere* (1975).

[31] S. L. Engerman, 'The Legacy of Slavery', unpublished paper submitted to *Duke University Symposium*, February 1978, 1–23.

[32] S. L. Engerman, 'Economic Adjustments for Emancipation in the United States and British West Indies', *Journal of Interdisciplinary History*, XIII (1982), 191–220.

[33] E. D. Fite, *Social and Industrial Conditions in the North During the Civil War* (1909, reprinted 1963).

[34] P. W. FitzRandolph, 'The Rural Furnishing Merchant in the Post-Bellum South United States: A study in Spatial Economics', *Journal of Economic History*, XLI (1981), 187–8.

[35] B. L. Fladeland, 'Compensated Emancipation: A Rejected Alternative', *Journal of Southern History*, XLII (1976), 170–85.

[36] H. W. Fleisig, 'Slavery and the Supply of Agricultural Labour and the Industrialization of the South', *Journal of Economic History*, XXXVI (1976), 572–97.

[37] R. W. Fogel and S. L. Engerman, 'The Economics of Slavery' in *The Reinterpretation of American Economic History* (1971).

[38] R. W. Fogel and S. L. Engerman, 'A Model for the Explanation of Industrial Expansion During the Nineteenth Century: With an application to the American Iron Industry', in R. W. Fogel and S. L. Engerman (eds), *The Reinterpretation of American Economic History* (1971).

[39] R. W. Fogel and S. L. Engerman, *Time on the Cross* (1974).

[40] R. W. Fogel and S. L. Engerman, 'Explaining the Relative Efficiency of Slave Agriculture in the Antebellum South', *American Economic Review*, LXVII (1977), 275–96.

[41] R. W. Fogel and S. L. Engerman, 'Explaining the Relative Efficiency of Slave Agriculture in the Antebellum South: Reply', *American Economic Review*, LXX (1980), 672–90.

[42] E. Foner, *Politics and Ideology in the Age of the Civil War* (1980).

[43] R. E. Gallman, 'The Structure of the Cotton Economy of the Antebellum South', *Agricultural History*, XLIV (1970), 5–23.

[44] R. E. Gallman, 'Slavery and Southern Economic Growth'. *Southern Economic Journal*, 45 (4) (1979), 1009–13.

[45] P. Gates, *Agriculture and the Civil War* (1965).

[46] E. D. Genovese, *The Political Economy of Slavery* (1967).

[47] D. T. Gilchrist and W. D. Lewis (eds), *Economic Change in the Civil War Era* (1965).

[48] C. Goldin, 'The Economics of Emancipation', *Journal of Economic History*, XXXIII (1973), 66–85.

[49] C. Goldin and F. Lewis, 'The Economic Cost of the American Civil War: Estimates and Implications', *Journal of Economic History*, XXXV (1975), 299–327.

[50] C. Goldin *Urban Slavery in the American South 1820–60* (1976).

[51] C. Goldin and F. Lewis, 'The Post-Bellum Recovery of the South and the Cost of the Civil War: Comment', *Journal of Economic History*, XXXVIII (1978), 487–92.

[52] C. Goldin, 'N Kinds of Freedom: An Introduction to the Issues', *Explorations in Economic History*, 16, (1979), 8–30.

[53] D. F. Gordon and G. M. Walton, 'A Theory of Regenerative

Growth and the Experience of Post World War II West Germany' in R. L. Ransom *et al.* (eds), *Exploration in the New Economic History* (1982), 169–92.

[54] G. Gunderson, 'The Origin of the American Civil War', *Journal of Economic History*, XXXIV (1974) 915–51.

[55] G. Gunderson, *A New Economic History of America* (1976).

[56] H. Gutman, *The Black Family in Slavery and Freedom* (1976).

[57] H. Gutman and R. Sutch, 'Sambo Makes Good, or Were Slaves Imbued with the Protestant Work Ethic?' in [17, 55–89].

[58] S. Hahn, *The Roots of Southern Populism* (1983).

[59] G. Hawke, 'The United States Tariff and Industrial Protection in the Late Nineteenth Century', *Economic History Review*, XXVIII (1975), 84–99.

[60] R. Higgs, 'Race Tenure and Resource Allocation in Southern Agriculture', *Journal of Economic History*, XXXIII (1973), 149–70.

[61] R. Higgs, *Competition and Coercion: Blacks in the American Economy, 1865–1914* (1977).

[62] R. Higgs, 'Accumulation of Property by Southern Blacks Before World War I', *American Economic Review*, LXXII (1982).

[63] R. Higgs and L. J. Alston, 'Contractual Mix in Southern Agriculture since the Civil War: Facts, Hypotheses and Tests', *Journal of Economic History*, XLII (1982), 327–54.

[64] J. Hughes, *American Economic History* (1983).

[65] J. James, 'The Development of the National Money Market', *Journal of Economic History*, XXXVI (1976), 878–97.

[66] J. James, *Money and Capital Markets in Postbellum America* (1978).

[67] J. James, 'Public Debt Policy and Nineteenth Century American Economic Growth' (unpublished paper University of Virginia Economics Department, 1981).

[68] J. James, 'Financial Underdevelopment in the Post-Bellum South', *Journal of Interdisciplinary History*, Winter (1981), 443–54.

[69] R. A. Kessel and A. A. Alchian, 'Real Wages in the North During the Civil War: Mitchell's Data Reinterpreted', in R. W. Fogel and S. L. Engerman, *The Reinterpretation of American Economic History*, (1971), 459–67.

[70] J. M. Kousser, 'Progressivism for Middle Class Whites Only',

Journal of Southern History, May (1980), 169–84.

[71] S. Kuznets, *Post War Economic Growth* (1964).

[72] W. A. Lewis, *Economic Survey, 1919–39* (1949).

[73] J. Mandle, 'The Plantation States as a Sub-Region of the Post-Bellum South', *Journal of Economic History*, XXXIV (1974), 732–8.

[74] J. Mandle, *The Roots of Black Poverty* (1978).

[75] M. Marable, 'The Politics of Black Land Tenure', *Agricultural History*, VIII (1979), 140–54.

[76] R. Margo, 'Race Differences in Public School Expenditures', *Social Science History*, 6 (1982), 9–31.

[77] R. McGuire and R. Higgs, 'Cotton Corn and Risk:Another View', *Explorations in Economic History*, 14 (1977), 167–82.

[78] J. M. McPherson, *The Struggle for Equality: Abolitionists and the Negro in the Civil War and Reconstruction* (1964).

[79] J. M. McPherson, *Ordeal by Fire: The Civil War and Reconstruction* (1982).

[80] J. Metzer, 'Rational Management, Modern Business Practices and Economies of Scale in the Ante-Bellum Southern Plantations', *Explorations in Economic History*, 12 (1975), 123–50.

[81] National Bureau of Economic Research, *Output, Employment and Productivity in the United States after 1800*, vol. 30 (1966).

[82] D. A. Novak, *The Wheel of Servitude* (1978).

[83] J. Oakes, *The Ruling Race: A History of American Slaveholders* (1982).

[84] C. F. Oubre, *Forty Acres and a Mule* (1978).

[85] W. N. Parker, 'The South in the National Economy, 1865–1970', *Southern Economic Journal*, 46 (1980), 1019–46.

[86] G. Porter and H. Livesay, *Merchants and Manufacturers* (1971).

[87] B. Poulson, *Economic History of the United States* (1981).

[88] R. L. Ransom and R. Sutch, 'Debt Peonage in the Cotton South After the Civil War', *Journal of Economic History*, XXXII (1972), 641–99.

[89] R. L. Ransom and R. Sutch, 'The Ex-Slave in the Post-Bellum South: the Economic Impact of Racism in a Market Environment', *Journal of Economic History*, XXXIII (1973), 131–48.

[90] R. L. Ransom and R. Sutch, 'The Impact of the Civil War and of the Emancipation of Southern Agriculture', *Explorations in Economic History*, 12 (1975), 1–28.

[91] R. L. Ransom and R. Sutch, 'The Lock-In Mechanism and Overproduction of Cotton in the Postbellum South', *Agricultural History*, 49, (1975), 405–25.

[92] R. L. Ransom and R. Sutch, *One Kind of Freedom* (1977).

[93] R. L. Ransom and R. Sutch, 'Sharecropping: Market Response or Mechanism of Race Control?' in [104].

[94] R. L. Ransom and R. Sutch, 'Growth and Welfare in the American South of the Nineteenth Century', *Explorations in Economic History*, 16 (1979), 207–35.

[95] R. L. Ransom and R. Sutch, 'Credit Merchandising in the Post Emancipation South, Conduct and Performance', *Explorations in Economic History*, 16 (1979a), 64–89.

[96] W. D. Rasmussen, 'The Civil War: A Catalyst of Agricultural Revolution', *Agricultural History*, 39 (1965), 187–95.

[97] S. Ratner, J. H. Soltow and R. Sylla, *The Evolution of the American Economy: Growth, Welfare and Decision-making* (1979).

[98] J. Reid, 'Sharecropping as an Understandable Market Response: The Post-Bellum South', *Journal of Economic History*, XXXIII (1973), 106–30.

[99] J. Reid, 'White Land, Black Labor and Agricultural Stagnation', *Explorations in Economic History*, 16 (1979), 31–55.

[100] J. L. Roark, *Masters without Slaves* (1977).

[101] W. L. Rose, 'What was Freedom's Price?' in [104].

[102] J. Rubin, 'The Limits of Agricultural Progress in the Nineteenth Century', *Agricultural History Review*, 49 (1975), 362–73.

[103] S. Salsbury, 'The Effect of the Civil War on American Industrial Development' in R. Andreano (ed.), *The Economic Impact of the Civil War* (1962).

[104] D. G. Sansing (ed.), *What was Freedom's Price?* (1978).

[105] R. Shlomowitz, 'The Origins of Southern Sharecropping', *Agricultural History*, LIII (1979), 557–75.

[106] H. Scheiber, 'Economic Change in the Civil War Era: An Analysis of Recent Studies', *Civil War History*, II (1965), 396–411.

[107] G. L. Sellers, 'The Incidence of the Civil War in the South', *Mississippi Valley Historical Review*, 14 (1927), 94–118.

[108] K. M. Stampp and L. F. Litwack, *Reconstruction: An Anthology of Revisionist Writings* (1969).

[109] L. Stone, 'The Results of the English Revolutions of the 17th

Century' in J. G. Pococke (ed.), *Three British Revolutions* (1980).

[110] P. Studenski and H. Kroos, *Financial History of the United States* (1952).

[111] R. Sylla, 'The United States, 1863–1913' in R. Cameron (ed.), *Banking and Economic Development* (1972).

[112] R. Sylla, *The American Capital Market 1846–1914* (1975).

[113] P. Temin, 'The Post-Bellum Recovery of the South and the Cost of the Civil War', *Journal of Economic History*, XXXVI (1976), 898–907.

[114] P. Temin, 'Reply to Goldin and Lewis', *Journal of Economic History*, XXXVIII (1978), 493.

[115] P. Temin, 'Freedom and Coercion: Notes on the Analysis of Debt Peonage in *One Kind of Freedom*', *Explorations in Economic History*, 16 (1979), 56–63.

[116] P. B. Trescott, 'Federal Government Receipts and Expenditure 1865–75', *Journal of Economic History*, XXVI (1966), 206–21.

[117] H. G. Vatter, *The Drive to Industrial Maturity: The United States Economy 1860–1914* (1975).

[118] R. K. Vedder, *The American Economy in Historical Perspective* (1976).

[119] M. Wayne, *The Reshaping of Plantation Society 1860–80* (1983).

[120] J. Weiner, 'Planter-Merchant Conflict in Reconstruction Alabama', *Past and Present*, 68 (1975), 73–94.

[121] J. Wiener, 'Planter Persistence and Social Change: Alabama, 1850–70', *Journal of Interdisciplinary History*, 7 (1976), 235–60.

[122] J. Wiener, *Social Origins of the New South: Alabama 1860–85* (1978).

[123] J. Wiener, 'Class Structure and Economic Development in the American South', *American Historical Review*, X (1979).

[124] J. G. Williamson, 'Watersheds and Turning Points: Conjectures on the Long Term Impact of Civil War Financing', *Journal of Economic History*, XXXIV (1974), 636–60.

[125] J. G. Williamson, *Late Nineteenth Century American Development* (1974).

[126] H. Woodman (ed.), *The Legacy of the American Civil War* (1973).

[127] H. Woodman, 'Sequel to Slavery: The New History Views on the Post-Bellum South', *Journal of Southern History*, 43 (1977), 523–54.

[128] H. Woodman, 'Post Civil War Agriculture and the Law', *Agricultural History*, LIII (1979), 319–37.

[129] H. Woodman, 'Post Bellum Social Change and its Effects on Marketing the South's Cotton Crop', *Agricultural History*, LV (1982), 211–27.

[130] C. V. Woodward, *Origins of the New South, 1877–1913* (1951).

[131] C. V. Woodward, 'The Price of Freedom' in [104].

[132] G. Wright, 'Comment on Papers by Reid, Ransom and Sutch and Higgs', *Journal of Economic History*, XXXIII (1973), 170–6.

[133] G. Wright, 'Cotton, Competition and the Post-Bellum Recovery of the American South', *Journal of Economic History*, XXXIV (1974), 610–35.

[134] G. Wright and H. Kunreuther, 'Cotton, Corn and Risk in the Nineteenth Century', *Journal of Economic History*, XXXV (1975), 526–51.

[135] G. Wright and H. Kunreuther, 'Cotton, Corn and Risk in the Nineteenth Century: A Reply', *Explorations in Economic History*, 14 (1977).

[136] G. Wright, *The Political Economy of the Cotton South*: (1978).

[137] G. Wright, 'The Strange Career of the New Southern Economic History', *Reviews in American History* (1982), 164–78.

[138] G. Wright, *Old South New South* (1986).

[139] R. Zevin, 'The Growth of Cotton Textile Production After 1815' in R. W. Fogel and S. L. Engerman (eds), *The Reinterpretation of American Economic History* (1971).

Index